HODDER GCSE HISTORY FOR

C000186796

THE USA, 1954–75
Conflict at home and abroad

Steve Waugh • John Wright

In order to ensure that this resource offers high-quality support for the associated Pearson qualification, it has been through a review process by the awarding body. This process confirms that this resource fully covers the teaching and learning content of the specification or part of a specification at which it is aimed. It also confirms that it demonstrates an appropriate balance between the development of subject skills, knowledge and understanding, in addition to preparation for assessment.

Endorsement does not cover any guidance on assessment activities or processes (e.g. practice questions or advice on how to answer assessment questions), included in the resource nor does it prescribe any particular approach to the teaching or delivery of a related course.

While the publishers have made every attempt to ensure that advice on the qualification and its assessment is accurate, the official specification and associated assessment guidance materials are the only authoritative source of information and should always be referred to for definitive guidance.

Pearson examiners have not contributed to any sections in this resource relevant to examination papers for which they have responsibility.

Examiners will not use endorsed resources as a source of material for any assessment set by Pearson.

Endorsement of a resource does not mean that the resource is required to achieve this Pearson qualification, nor does it mean that it is the only suitable material available to support the qualification, and any resource lists produced by the awarding body shall include this and other appropriate resources.

For JJ – '64 years...'

The publishers would like to thank the following for permission to reproduce copyright material.

Every effort has been made to trace all copyright holders, but if any have been inadvertently overlooked, the publishers will be pleased to make the necessary arrangements at the first opportunity.

Although every effort has been made to ensure that website addresses are correct at time of going to press, Hodder Education cannot be held responsible for the content of any website mentioned in this book. It is sometimes possible to find a relocated web page by typing in the address of the home page for a website in the URL window of your browser.

Hachette UK's policy is to use papers that are natural, renewable and recyclable products and made from wood grown in sustainable forests. The logging and manufacturing processes are expected to conform to the environmental regulations of the country of origin.

Orders: please contact Bookpoint Ltd, 130 Milton Park, Abingdon, Oxon OX14 4SB. Telephone: (44) 01235 827720. Fax: (44) 01235 400454. Email education@bookpoint.co.uk Lines are open from 9 a.m. to 5 p.m., Monday to Saturday, with a 24-hour message answering service. You can also order through our website: www.hoddereducation.co.uk

ISBN: 9781471861956

© Steve Waugh John Wright 2015

First published in 2016 by
Hodder Education,
An Hachette UK Company
Carmelite House
50 Victoria Embankment
London EC4Y 0DZ

www.hoddereducation.co.uk

Impression number   10 9 8 7 6 5 4 3

Year   2020 2019 2018

All rights reserved. Apart from any use permitted under UK copyright law, no part of this publication may be reproduced or transmitted in any form or by any means, electronic or mechanical, including photocopying and recording, or held within any information storage and retrieval system, without permission in writing from the publisher or under licence from the Copyright Licencing Agency Limited. Further details of such licences (for reprographic reproduction) may be obtained from the Copyright Licensing Agency limited, Saffron House, 6–10 Kirby Street, London EC1N 8TS.

Cover photo © The Granger Collection, NYC / TopFoto/© Paul Schutzer/The LIFE Picture Collection/Getty Images

Illustrations by DC Graphic Design Ltd

Typeset in ITC Legacy Serif 10/12pt by DC Graphic Design Ltd

Printed in India

A catalogue record for this title is available from the British Library.

CONTENTS

Introduction

About the course

During this course you must study four studies:

- A thematic study and historic environment
- A period study
- A British depth study
- A modern depth study.

These studies are assessed through three examination papers:

- For Paper 1 you have one hour and 15 minutes to answer questions on your chosen theme.
- In Paper 2 you have one hour and 45 minutes to answer questions on a depth study and a British period study.
- In Paper 3 you have one hour and 20 minutes to answer source questions on one modern depth study.

Modern Depth Study (Paper 3)

There are four options in the modern depth study unit. You have to study one. The three options are:

- Russia and the Soviet Union, 1917–41
- Weimar and Nazi Germany, 1918–39
- Mao's China 1945–76
- The USA, 1954–75: Conflict at home and abroad

About the book

The book is divided into four key topics.

- **Key topic 1** examines the development of the civil rights movement in the years 1954–60 including progress in education with the *Brown v Topeka* and Little Rock cases, the Montgomery Bus Boycott and the opposition to the movement.
- **Key topic 2** explains developments in the civil rights movement in the years 1960–75, especially the activities of Martin Luther King between 1963 and 1968, including the significance of his assassination, and Malcom X and the emergence of the Black Power Movement.
- **Key topic 3** concentrates on US involvement in the Vietnam War, including early involvement under Eisenhower and Kennedy and increasing involvement under Johnson and Nixon.
- **Key topic 4** examines reactions to the war in the USA including supporters and opponents of the war, how the war ended and its impact on the USA and the reasons for the failure of the USA in the war.

Each chapter in this book:

- contains activities – some develop the historical skills you will need, others are exam-style questions that give you the opportunity to practise exam skills.
- gives step-by-step guidance, model answers and advice on how to answer particular question types in Paper 3.
- defines key terms and highlights glossary terms in bold and colour the first time they appear in each key topic.

About Paper 3

Paper 3 is a test of:

- knowledge and understanding of the key developments in the USA, 1954–75
- the ability to answer brief and extended essay questions
- the ability to answer source and interpretation questions.

You have to answer the following types of questions. Each requires you to demonstrate different historical skills:

- **Inference** – making two supported inferences.
- **Causation** – explaining why something happened.
- **Utility** – evaluating the usefulness of sources.
- **Interpretation** – explaining what differences there are between two interpretations and why they differ. Making a judgement on a view given by one of the interpretations.

On page 5 is a set of exam-style questions (without the sources). You will be given step-by-step guidance in Chapters 2–13 on how best to approach and answer these types of questions.

Paper 3 Modern depth study
Option 33 The USA, 1954–75: conflict at home and abroad

This is an **inference** question – you have to make two inferences and support each with details from the source.

1 Give **two** things you can infer from Source A about the Freedom Riders.

   a) What I can infer:

     ....

     ....

     Details in the source that tell me this:

     ....

     ....

   b) What I can infer:

     ....

     ....

     Details in the source that tell me this:

     ....

     ....

(Total for Question 1 = 4 marks)

This is a **causation** question – which gives you two points. You should develop at least three clear points and explain the importance of each of them.

2 Explain why there was progress in the civil rights movement in the 1950s.

> You may use the following in your answer:
> - *Brown v Topeka* (1954)
> - The Montgomery Bus Boycott (1955–56)
>
> You **must** also use information of your own.

(Total for Question 2 = 12 marks)

This is a **utility** question – it is asking you to decide how useful each source is.

3 a) Study Sources B and C. How useful are Sources B and C for an enquiry into the reasons for the failure of the USA to win in Vietnam? Explain your answer, using Sources B and C and your knowledge of the historical context.

(8)

This is an **interpretation** question – you have to explain one main difference between the two interpretations.

b) Study Interpretations 1 and 2. They give different views about the reasons for the failure of the USA to win in Vietnam. What is the main difference between the views? Explain your answer, using details from both interpretations.

(4)

This is an **interpretation** question – you have to explain why these interpretations differ.

c) Suggest **one** reason why Interpretations 1 and 2 give different views about the reasons for the failure of the USA to win in Vietnam. You may use sources B and C to help explain your answer.

(4)

Up to 4 marks of the total for part (d) will be awarded for spelling, punctuation, grammar and use of specialist terminology.

This is an **interpretation judgement** question – you are asked to make a judgement on a view given by one of the interpretations.

d) How far do you agree with Interpretation 2 about the reasons for the failure of the USA to win in Vietnam? Explain your answer, using both interpretations, and your knowledge of the historical context.

(20)

(Total for spelling, punctuation and grammar, and the use of specialist terminology = 4 marks)

(Total for Question 3 = 36 marks)
(Total for Paper = 52 marks)

The development of the civil rights movement, 1954–60

This key topic examines the major developments in the civil rights movement from 1954 to 1960. The chapters cover vital issues such as education, segregation on transport, growth of civil rights organisations and opposition to progress, especially in the South.

Each chapter within this key topic explains a key issue and examines important lines of enquiry, as outlined below.

There will also be guidance on how to answer the following question types:

- Understanding interpretations (pages 13)
- How to answer the first question on interpretations – what is the main difference between the views (pages 22).

CHAPTER 1 THE POSITION OF BLACK AMERICANS IN THE EARLY 1950S

- Segregation, discrimination and voting rights in the Southern states.
- The work of civil rights organisations, including the NAACP and CORE.

CHAPTER 2 PROGRESS IN EDUCATION IN THE 1950S

- The key features of the *Brown v Topeka* case (1954).
- The immediate and long-term significance of the case.
- The significance of the events at Little Rock High School, 1957.

CHAPTER 3 THE MONTGOMERY BUS BOYCOTT AND ITS IMPACT, 1955–60

- Causes and events of the Montgomery Bus Boycott. The significance of Rosa Parks.
- Reasons for the success and importance of the boycott. The Supreme Court ruling. The Civil Rights Act 1957.
- The significance of the leadership of Martin Luther King. The setting up of the SCLC.

CHAPTER 4 OPPOSITION TO THE CIVIL RIGHTS MOVEMENT

- The Ku Klux Klan and violence, including the murder of Emmet Till in 1955.
- Opposition to desegregation in the South. The setting up of White Citizens' Councils.
- Congress and the 'Dixiecrats'.

TIMELINE 1954–60

1954	*Brown v Topeka* case
1955 August	Emmett Till murdered
1955 December	Beginning of the Montgomery Bus Boycott
1956	Bus Boycott successful, segregation on buses ends
1957 January	Southern Christian Leadership Conference (SCLC) formed by Martin Luther King, who also becomes president
1957 September	Little Rock High School
1957 September	Civil Rights Act passed

1 The position of black Americans in the early 1950s

Racial discrimination was a common feature of everyday life in the USA in the early 1950s. There were laws which permitted segregation and there was discrimination in all walks of life denying African Americans equality with their fellow white citizens. The Second World War had provided some opportunities for African Americans and, as a result, a few aspects of life improved. The mobilisation of US industry in the 1940s created employment, and hundreds of thousands of African Americans moved from the South to the North where there were higher wages. Better jobs and higher pay continued into the early 1950s but this was not so in the South. Despite some advances, African Americans received poor education, had poor housing, had the worst paid jobs and healthcare was not as good as their white counterparts. Though African Americans could vote, there were many restrictions to prevent them voting. Civil rights organisations such as NAACP and CORE followed policies to put right these issues.

1.1 Segregation, discrimination and voting rights in the Southern States

At the time the Second World War ended, there were a host of state laws which segregated African Americans from whites in daily life, known as the 'Jim Crow' laws. The worst cases were in the Southern states where the majority of African Americans lived (see Source A). Inter-marriage was against the law in most Southern states and Southern towns were segregated into black and white areas. Not only were residential areas segregated but public places such as hospitals, cinemas, shops, hotels, parks, libraries and theatres were too. Transport was also segregated but it was in education that this policy caused greatest concern.

African American children could legally be educated in separate schools (see page 10), provided that the schools provided an education which was equal to that of white children. This was following the *Plessey v Ferguson* case in 1896 when the Supreme Court had judged that if separate conditions for blacks and whites were equal, then segregation was constitutional. The idea of 'separate but equal' grew and this gave the policy of segregation a clear basis.

Discrimination

Racial discrimination is the practice of treating a person less fairly because of their race or skin colour. As a result of segregation, there developed widespread discrimination which meant African Americans experienced problems in housing, jobs and educational opportunity. Poor opportunities and discrimination led to jobs of lower status for African Americans, with large numbers being restricted to menial and unskilled positions. Economic discrimination meant that African Americans received lower wages and they were therefore unable to afford houses in better neighbourhoods. Discrimination and segregation produced a vicious circle which resulted in continued oppression.

▲ Source A Segregated drinking fountains in the American South

Voting rights

In addition to segregation and discrimination, African Americans had to endure being disenfranchised in a number of ways. The Fifteenth Amendment to the Constitution granted African American men the right to vote by declaring that the 'right of citizens of the United States to vote shall not be denied or abridged by the United States or by any state on account of race, colour, or previous condition of servitude.' However, many states introduced poll taxes and literacy tests which were designed to prevent African Americans from voting. Most African Americans were unable to pay the poll tax because they were too poor.

The literacy tests required voters to prove that they could read (see Source B). Many could not read or write because there were few schools and those that existed were of very poor quality. In the case of those African Americans who had basic literacy skills, particularly difficult extracts would be selected. In Alabama, in order to register to vote, a person had to read out loud to the registrar a section of the constitution (and in some cases verbally interpret it to his satisfaction). Then the applicant had to write out a section of the constitution. After that, there were written questions that were impossible to answer, such as 'How many bubbles in a bar of soap?' Even if the literacy tests were passed, African Americans would then be subjected to violence and intimidation to prevent them casting their vote.

▼ **Source B** Part of a literacy test from the state of Louisiana, circa 1964

24. Print a word that looks the same whether it is printed frontwards or backwards.

25. Write down on the line provided, what you read in the triangle below.

26. In the third square below, write the second letter of the fourth word.

27. Write right from the left to the right as you see it spelled here.

28. Divide a vertical line in two equal parts by bisecting it with a curved horizontal line that is only straight at its spot bisection of the vertical.

29. Write every other word in this first line and print every third word in same line (original type smaller and first line ended at coma) but capitalize the fifth word that you write.

30. Draw five circles that one common inter-locking part.

ACTIVITIES ?

1 Explain what is meant by the term 'Jim Crow Laws'.

2 Which do you consider to be the most damaging feature of segregation? Explain your answer.

3 Study Source B.
   a) Complete the questions and check the answers with your teacher. See how many in the class scored full marks.
   b) Construct an argument saying why literacy tests should be banned.

Practice questions

1 How useful are Sources A (page 7) and B for an enquiry into the position of black Americans? Explain your answer, using Sources A and B and your knowledge of the historical context. *(For guidance, see pages 71–73.)*

2 Give two things you can infer from Source C about the leaders of the NAACP. *(For guidance, see page 79.)*

3 Explain why black Americans were treated as inferior in the early 1950s.

You may use the following in your answer:
- Segregation
- Voting rights

You **must** also use information of your own.

(For guidance, see pages 94–95.)

1.2 The work of civil rights organisations

Despite the issues facing African Americans before 1954, there were many activists who tried to improve civil rights. The **Congress of Racial Equality (CORE)** and the **National Association for the Advancement of Colored People (NAACP)** were two prominent pressure groups which both sought to end discriminatory practices. There were some successes. In 1948, the NAACP pressured President Truman into signing the Executive Order that banned discrimination by the **Federal Government**. Two years later, the head of the NAACP's legal department, Thurgood Marshall, won his case in the Supreme Court for state universities to provide equal facilities for all students. However, the two groups lacked political influence and people with charisma to push civil rights to the forefront of US politics.

Congress of Racial Equality (CORE)

The Congress of Racial Equality (CORE) was founded by James Farmer, a young black American activist (see Source C). CORE was inspired by the non-violent tactics of Mahatma Gandhi in India. It employed the idea of **sit-ins** (see page 28) at cinemas and restaurants to highlight the issue of segregation, which led to the end of this practice in some cities in northern states in the late 1940s. CORE also began to demand the end of segregation on transport. Though quiet in the later 1950s, CORE became more prominent in the 1960s during the Freedom Rides (page 30) and the Freedom Summer (see page 42).

National Association for the Advancement of Colored People (NAACP)

The NAACP had been founded in 1909 by a group of leading black intellectuals. The organisation was multi-racial and W.E.B. du Bois was a leading member. Du Bois was one of the most important figures in the campaign for civil rights in the first half of the twentieth century. He was an intellectual and an activist. The main aim of the NAACP was 'to ensure the political, educational, social and economic equality of rights of all persons and to eliminate racial hatred and racial discrimination'. The NAACP sought to use all legal means to achieve equality. However, it was often criticised for working within the system by some of its own members, who wanted a more robust approach to protest.

Growing awareness of discrimination and its injustice led to a growth in membership of the NAACP – from 50,000 in 1940 to 600,000 by 1946. Many of the new members were professional people, but there were also many new urban workers. The NAACP played an important part in the civil rights movement because it raised the profile of issues not only within the black community but also the white one.

Moreover, it encouraged many black Americans to become active in the quest for civil rights.

The extent of change by the 1950s

By the end of the 1940s, those seeking improved civil rights had made only modest gains. There had been some progress in employment and the armed forces, and many blacks had become more active in campaigning for civil rights. On the other hand, discrimination and segregation remained a way of life in the Southern states, while the migration of many black Americans to the industrial cities of the North had created greater racial tension.

In the 1950s, the NAACP became involved in the *Brown v Topeka* case (see page 10) and the Montgomery Bus Boycott (see pages 14–19). In 1957, a third African American civil rights group was founded, the **Southern Christian Leadership Conference (SCLC)** (see page 20), adding momentum to the demand for change in the USA.

> **ACTIVITY** ?
>
> Carry out your own research about Mahatma Gandhi and his tactics.

▲ **Source C** Leaders of the NAACP in 1956, from left to right: Henry L. Moon, Director of Public Relations, Roy Wilkins, General Secretary, Herbert Hill, Labour Secretary and Thurgood Marshall, Special Legal Counsel

2 Progress in education

The 1950s saw significant developments in the civil rights movement, more especially in education. The *Brown v Topeka* case not only challenged segregation in education, particularly in the Southern States of the USA, but also highlighted the importance of the Supreme Court in improving the position of black Americans. However, the case also encouraged opposition in the South and led to events at Little Rock High School in 1957, which in turn, brought direct intervention from President Eisenhower.

2.1 The *Brown v Topeka* case, 1954

One of the main reasons for the lack of progress for black Americans in the South was due to **segregation** and **discrimination** limiting educational opportunities for black Americans. Segregation meant that black Americans were not allowed to attend white schools, and in the black schools the facilities and resources were far inferior to those provided for white Americans. South Carolina, for example, spent three times more on white-only schools than black-only schools. Figure 2.1 shows the areas where segregation of schools was a matter of state legislation before 1957.

The first case to challenge segregation did not originate in the South, but in the Midwest state of Kansas. Linda Brown's parents wanted her to attend a neighbourhood school rather than the school for black Americans, which was some distance away. Lawyers from the NAACP (led by Thurgood Marshall) presented evidence to the Supreme Court, stating that separate education created low self-esteem and was psychologically harmful. Moreover, the evidence also pointed out that educational achievement was restricted because of this policy. The process took 18 months and the decision to ban school segregation was announced on 17 May 1954. Chief Justice Warren of the Supreme Court gave a closing judgement (see Source A).

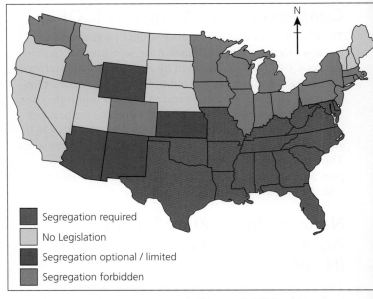

▲ **Figure 2.1** Educational segregation in the USA before the *Brown v Topeka* case

Legend:
- Segregation required
- No Legislation
- Segregation optional / limited
- Segregation forbidden

Source A From the closing judgment of Chief Justice Warren of the Supreme Court at the end of the *Brown v Topeka* case

Separating white and colored children in schools had a detrimental effect upon colored children. The impact is greater when it has the sanction of the law; for the separating of the races is usually interpreted as denoting the inferiority of the Negro group ... We conclude that in the field of public education the doctrine of 'separate but equal' has no place. Separate educational facilities are inherently unequal.

The significance of *Brown v Topeka*

Despite the judgement ruling against segregated education, it did not specify how integration should be carried out – apart from a vague notion of 'at the earliest possible speed'. Some areas began to desegregate and by 1957, more than 300,000 black children were attending schools that had formerly been segregated. Nevertheless, there were 2.4 million black Southern children who were still being educated in 'Jim Crow' schools.

Moreover, there were many states, especially in the South, that took deliberate measures to keep separate schools. President Eisenhower did not step in to enforce integration because he did not want to cause further opposition in the South. He said it would be 'just plain nuts' if he used force to carry out the Brown decision.

The Ku Klux Klan (see page 23) had been extremely popular in the 1920s and now began to re-emerge. Some parents joined White Citizens' Councils (see page 25), which aimed to maintain segregation. More than 100 Southern senators and congressmen signed the Southern Manifesto, a document that opposed racial integration in education. Over the next two years, Southern state legislatures passed more than 450 laws and resolutions aimed at preventing the Brown decision being enforced.

Some of the Southern states acted as they did because they saw the Federal Government as acting in a dictatorial manner, over-ruling their independence. In this way, they were able to say their actions were political not racist.

Despite the decision of the Supreme Court and the open hostility to the *Brown v Topeka* case, President Eisenhower did little to encourage integration. He was forced into action in 1957 by events at Little Rock High School in Arkansas.

THE AUTHERINE LUCY CASE

In 1956, the University of Alabama accepted a black student, Autherine Lucy, under a government court order that had been secured by the NAACP. Many white students rioted and the university authorities removed her. She was forbidden to re-enter the university. It was 1963 before black Americans were finally allowed to study there.

ACTIVITIES ?

1 Study Figure 2.1 (page 10). What does this map show you about segregation in education in the USA before the Brown decision?

2 What reasons did Chief Justice Warren give in his dismissal of the Jim Crow laws in Source A?

3 Study Source C. Working in pairs add two captions for the photograph:
   ■ One for a black civil rights newspaper
   ■ The other for a Southern white newspaper

4 Did the *Brown v Topeka* case bring progress for the civil rights movement? Copy the table below and complete the boxes, explaining your answers.

Yes, because:	No, because:

Practice questions

1 Give two things you can infer from Source A about the *Brown v Topeka* case. (*For guidance, see page 79.*)

2 How useful are Sources A and B for an enquiry into the *Brown v Topeka* case? Explain your answer, using Sources A and B and your knowledge of the historical context. (*For guidance, see pags 71–73.*)

▲ **Source B** The front page of the Topeka State Journal following the Supreme Court's Decision

▲ **Source C** Three NAACP lawyers, (from left) George E.C. Hayes, Thurgood Marshall and James Nabrit Jr, celebrating after the *Brown v Topeka* verdict

2.2 Little Rock High School, 1957

After the *Brown v Topeka* decision, Little Rock High School, Arkansas, decided to allow nine black students to enrol there. On 3 September 1957, the nine – led by Elizabeth Eckford – tried to enrol but were prevented by the State governor, Orval Faubus, who ordered Arkansas State National Guardsmen to block the students' entry. Faubus said there were threats of public disorder if black students tried to enrol. The following day, 4 September, the National Guard was removed by order of Faubus, and the nine students ran the gauntlet of a vicious white crowd which numbered almost 1,000. At midday, the students went home under police guard because their safety could not be guaranteed.

President Eisenhower had to act. He took control of the National Guard and used them and federal troops to protect the black students for the rest of the school year. Despite the president's intervention, Governor Faubus closed all Arkansas schools the following year, to prevent integration. Many white and most black students had no schooling for a year. Schools in Arkansas only reopened in 1959 following a Supreme Court ruling.

▲ **Source D** Black American students arriving at Little Rock High School in a US army car, 1957

▲ **Source E** Demonstrators against integration in schools in Arkansas, 1959

Why was Little Rock significant?

The events at Little Rock were significant for a number of reasons:

- It involved the president, thus demonstrating that civil rights was an issue that could no longer be ignored.
- It demonstrated that states would be overruled by the Federal Government when necessary.
- The demonstrations were seen on television and in newspapers across the world. The USA was embarrassed to be seen as an oppressive nation when it was criticising communist countries for not allowing their citizens basic human rights.
- It came at a time when the Soviet Union had launched its sputnik satellite and gave the Soviet media the opportunity to claim not only technological superiority but also moral superiority over the USA.
- Many US citizens saw, for the first time, the racial hatred that existed in the Southern states.
- It did help to moderate some of the views held by white Americans at the time because Little Rock had highlighted the continued racism, especially in the Southern states.
- Events like those at Little Rock High School led black activists to realise that reliance on the federal courts was not enough to secure change. The issue of civil rights was now at the heart of US politics.

ACTIVITIES ❓

1 Why do you think that education played such an important part in the struggle for civil rights in the 1950s?

2 Did events at Little Rock High School bring progress for the civil rights movement? Copy the table below and complete the boxes, explaining your answers.

Yes, because:	No, because:

3 What can you learn from Source E about attitudes to integration in the USA in 1959?

Practice question

Explain why there was progress in education for black Americans in the 1950s.

You may use the following in your answer:
- *Brown v Topeka*
- Little Rock High School

You **must** also use information of your own.

(For guidance, see pages 94–95.)

2.3 What are interpretations of history?

You will have to answer three questions about interpretations in the examination. These are:

- What is the main difference between these interpretations?
- Why are these interpretations different?
- How far do you agree with the view given by one of the interpretations?

An interpretation of history is a view given of the past – an event, movement, role of an individual and so on, written at a later date. It could be a view given by a historian, from a textbook or a history website. The writer has the benefit of hindsight and is able to consult a variety of sources of evidence to give their view of what took place.

There are different interpretations about a past event or person because the writer could focus on or give emphasis to a different aspect of a past event or person, or they may have consulted different sources from the past. The writer will carefully choose words and select or omit certain details to emphasise this view. The fact that there are different interpretations of the past does not necessarily mean that one of them is wrong. The two writers might simply have used different sources but they might also have used the same sources and reached different conclusions.

Your first task is to identify the view that is given by the interpretation of the event or person. Here is an interpretation of the passing of the Civil Rights Bill:

> **Interpretation 1 From The History Learning website**
>
> The Civil Rights Bill's success in passing Congress owed much to the murder of Kennedy. The mood of the public in general would not have allowed any obvious deliberate attempts to damage 'Kennedy's Bill'. Johnson played the obvious card – how could anybody vote against an issue so dear to the late president's heart? How could anybody be so unpatriotic? Johnson simply appealed to the nation – still traumatised by Kennedy's murder.

The view that is given here is:

> This interpretation gives the view that the passing of the Bill was because of the death of Kennedy. It uses phrases such as 'owed much' and 'damage Kennedy's Bill' to show this view. It also focuses on the idea of 'patriotism' and 'appealing to the nation'.

Here is a second interpretation of the passing of the Civil Rights Bill:

> **Interpretation 2 Adapted from the Youth for Human Rights website**
>
> In 1963, King guided peaceful mass demonstrations that the white police force countered with police dogs and fire hoses and this generated newspaper headlines throughout the world. Subsequent mass demonstrations ... culminated in a march that attracted more than 250,000 protestors to Washington, DC, where King delivered his famous 'I have a dream' speech ... So powerful was the movement he inspired, that Congress enacted the Civil Rights Act in 1964. That same year King himself was honoured with the Nobel Peace Prize.

And here is an interpretation of the effects of the desegregation campaign of the 1950s:

> **Interpretation 3 From The Twentieth Century World by John Martell, published in 1985**
>
> The desegregation campaign did not result in many immediate benefits for African Americans. It was important in another way: it marked the start of the civil rights movement that was to grow in importance during the 1960s and 1970s. Their often bitter experiences during the desegregation events of the 1950s brought African Americans together in a way never achieved before.

ACTIVITIES

Read Interpretation 1 and the information underneath it. This outlines the view it gives of the passing of the Civil rights Act and the evidence it uses. Now try answering the questions below on Interpretations 2 and 3 in a similar way.

Interpretation 2
1 What view does it give of the passing of the Civil Rights Bill?
2 What evidence from the interpretation supports this view?

Interpretation 3
3 What view does it give of the effects of the desegregation campaign?
4 What evidence from the interpretation supports this view?

You will be given advice in the following chapters as to how to answer these questions.

3 The Montgomery Bus Boycott and its impact, 1955–60

Education and public transport were the two immediate areas of contention for African Americans in the early 1950s. Segregation on public transport in the USA had long been a problem for black Americans. Attempts to end this had found some success in the early 1950s in Baton Rouge, Louisiana, where, following a ten-day bus boycott, black Americans were allowed to board buses from back to front and whites from front to back. However, blacks were still prohibited from sitting with or in front of white passengers. The transport issue came to a head in Montgomery, Alabama, after the arrest of Rosa Parks in December 1955. The boycott raised national awareness of segregation and the protest at last produced a charismatic leader who could raise the profile of racial issues and also stand as an articulate voice for African Americans. This was Martin Luther King.

3.1 Causes and events of the Montgomery Bus Boycott

The rules about **segregation** on public transport in Montgomery were particularly harsh:

- Black Americans had to follow the instructions of the white drivers.
- The front part of the bus was reserved for whites at all times.
- Black Americans had to fill the bus from the back.
- Black Americans could not sit next to whites and had to stand even if there was a vacant seat in the whites section.
- If a white person boarded the bus and all white seats were taken, black people had to give up their seats.

In March 1955 there had been a case where Claudette Colvin, a young black girl, had been arrested for refusing to give up her seat to a white person. The **NAACP** (see page 9) in Montgomery had considered challenging the segregation laws for some time, but decided to wait for a stronger case (Colvin became pregnant during the time the NAACP was considering her case and, as she was unmarried, it was felt that this would be seized on by white opponents). The opportunity came on Thursday 1 December 1955, when Rosa Parks refused to give up her seat to a white man. She was subsequently arrested and from this point the situation escalated into a crisis. On the day after Parks' arrest, Jo Ann Robinson, leader of the Montgomery Women's Political Council, and some students printed thousands of leaflets encouraging people to boycott buses (see Source B).

Initially, Robinson decided to hold a one-day boycott on Monday 5 December, the day of Parks' trial.

THE SIGNIFICANCE OF ROSA PARKS

- Parks was the secretary of the local NAACP and knew many influential local activists.
- Rosa was well thought of and highly respected in her community.
- She knew she might lose her job as a seamstress if she challenged the segregation law. When news emerged of her arrest, she was sacked by her employer, Montgomery Fair Department store.
- She endured harassment during the whole of the boycott but never spoke out against it. Her husband also lost his job during the boycott and they eventually moved to Detroit.
- She was a symbol of the struggle in Montgomery and became known as 'the mother of the civil rights movement'.
- In 1999, *TIME* magazine named Rosa Parks on its list of 'The 20 Most Influential People of the 20th Century.'

▲ **Source A** Rosa Parks being fingerprinted in 1955

Preparation for the boycott

During the weekend prior to the bus boycott, local civil rights activists such as E.D. Nixon, Ralph Abernathy and Martin Luther King Jr became involved. (For more on Martin Luther King, his life and the significance of his leadership, see page 20.) They began to plan a rally for the evening of the trial and the local NAACP started preparing its legal challenge to the segregation laws. At the meeting, the Montgomery Improvement Association (MIA) was established to oversee the continuation and maintenance of the boycott and also to 'improve the general status of Montgomery, to improve race relations, and to uplift the general tenor of the community'. At this stage the demands of the protestors were limited, seeking only to end the policy of black Americans standing when white seats were vacant.

Source B Part of the leaflet used to encourage the bus boycott, December 1955

Another Negro woman has been arrested and thrown in jail because she refused to get up out of her seat on the bus for a white person to sit down.

This has to be stopped. Negroes have rights, too. Three quarters of the riders are Negroes, yet we are arrested, or have to stand when there are empty seats. If we do not do something to stop these arrests, they will continue. The next time it may be you, or your daughter, or mother.

This woman's case will come up on Monday. We are asking every Negro to stay off the buses Monday in protest of the arrest and trial. Don't ride the buses to work, to town, to school, or anywhere on Monday. If you work, take a cab, or walk. But please, children and grown-ups, don't ride the bus at all on Monday. Please stay off all buses Monday.

ACTIVITIES ?

1 What were the two most significant features of Rosa Parks' involvement in the Bus Boycott? Explain your answer.

2 Why did the Montgomery Bus Boycott begin in December 1955?

Practice question

Give two things you can infer from Source B about the leaders of the Montgomery Bus Boycott. (*For guidance, see page 79.*)

The events of the Montgomery Bus Boycott

It is thought that about 20,000 people were involved in the Monday bus boycott. During the evening of 5 December, some 7,000 people attended the planned rally and heard Martin Luther King make an inspirational speech. King was determined to follow the path of non-violence, even in the face of police and racist violence.

His speech explained that African Americans were extremely tired of being humiliated and oppressed in their own country. He said that the patience of African Americans may have seemed as if they did not mind the way they were treated, but now their patience was at an end. However, King was quick to point out that African Americans would not resort to violence, saying 'There will be no cross burnings ... we will be guided by law and order'. He emphasised that their cause would be that of persuasion.

Rosa Parks was fined $10 for the offence on the bus and $4 costs. The MIA then decided to continue the boycott until its demands were met. At this point, the Montgomery authorities made a huge error of judgement in refusing the moderates' demands. By doing so, they pushed King and the MIA to demand complete desegregation on buses.

▲ **Source C** Montgomery citizens walking to work during the boycott

▲ **Source D** Martin Luther King addressing leaders of the boycott. Rosa Parks is seated in the front row and on her right is Ralph Abernathy, a leading figure in the black community

ACTIVITIES

1 What can you learn from Source D about Martin Luther King?

2 Why was King keen to put the emphasis on persuasion in his speech of 5 December 1955?

3 What did King mean when he said 'There will be no cross burnings'?

Practice questions

1 Give two things you can infer from Source C about the organisers of the boycott (*For further guidance, see page 79.*)

2 How useful are Sources C and D for an enquiry into the Montgomery Bus Boycott? Explain your answer, using Sources C and D and your knowledge of the historical context. (*For guidance, see pages 71–73.*)

Maintaining the boycott

Those boycotting the buses were helped during the first few days by black taxi companies charging only 10 cents per ride. However, within a few days, an obscure Montgomery City Law was used, which stated that the minimum taxi fare had to be 45 cents. Such a figure was too expensive for many black workers. As the boycott progressed, churches bought cars in order to take people to and from work (see Source G). This created problems because there had to be specific pick-up places for the workers, and while people were waiting to be picked up they were harassed by the police, who used local laws to try and prevent crowds gathering. The police also attempted to intimidate drivers and arrested many for minor traffic violations. However, the pooling of cars ensured that black Americans continued the boycott.

Intimidation tactics

Maintaining the boycott meant the boycotters faced continued intimidation. The Montgomery White Council led the organised opposition. Membership of this body swelled to almost 12,000 by March 1956, and its membership included some of Montgomery's leading city officials. In some cases the violence used against the boycotters was extreme. In January 1956, King's home was firebombed and his wife and young daughter only narrowly escaped injury. Other leaders had their homes firebombed during 1956.

The next step in intimidation came in February 1956, when about 90 of the leading figures – including King and Rosa Parks – were arrested for organising an illegal boycott (see Source E). Although they were found guilty, no charges were made after appeal.

Source F From Martin Luther King, *Stride Toward Freedom*, published in 1958. Here he is describing how he addressed the crowd of people who had gathered outside his house, which had been firebombed on 30 January 1956

I walked out to the porch and asked the crowd to come to order. In less than a moment there was complete silence. Quietly I told them that I was all right and that my wife and baby were all right. 'Now let's not become panicky,' I continued. 'If you have weapons, take them home; if you do not have them, please do not seek to get them. We cannot solve this problem through retaliatory violence. We must meet violence with non-violence. Remember the words of Jesus: "He who lives by the sword will perish by the sword".'

ACTIVITIES ?

1 Study Source E. What impression of Martin Luther King do you gain from this photograph?
2 What can you learn from Source F about those involved in the boycott? (Remember how to answer this type of question.)

▲ **Source E** Police photograph of Martin Luther King on his arrest in Montgomery, 22 February 1956

▲ **Source G** African Americans residents' carpool during the boycott, 1956

The Supreme Court ruling

As the boycott moved into the summer, the US national press covered events more closely, and this helped raise awareness of the issue of deep racial hatred in the South.

The MIA took the issue of segregation on transport to a federal district court on the basis that it was unconstitutional, citing the *Brown v Topeka* case (see page 10). The federal court accepted that segregation was unconstitutional. However, Montgomery city officials appealed and the case went to the Supreme Court. On 13 November 1956, the Supreme Court upheld the federal court's decision. The boycott had been successful. It formally came to an end on 20 December 1956 when King, Abernathy and other leaders travelled on an integrated bus.

> **Source H** Part of Martin Luther King's speech at a meeting in Montgomery 20 December 1956, the day the boycott formally ended.
>
> This is the time that we must show calm dignity and wise restraint. Emotions must not run wild. Violence must not come from any of us, for if we become victimized with violent intent, we will have walked in vain, and our twelve months of glorious dignity will be transformed into a time of gloomy catastrophe. As we go back to the buses let us be loving enough to turn an enemy into a friend. We must now move from protest to reconciliation. It is my firm conviction that God is working in Montgomery. Let all men of goodwill, both Negro and white, continue to work with Him. With this dedication we will be able to emerge from the bleak and desolate midnight of man's inhumanity to man to the bright and glittering daybreak of freedom and justice.

White reaction to the ruling

The **Ku Klux Klan's** (see page 23) response was to send carloads of its members around the black areas of Montgomery to try and intimidate the residents. The blacks simply waved at the hooded Klan. In early 1957, there were sniper attacks on some of the buses, King's home was attacked again and four churches were bombed, but the white backlash gradually diminished.

ACTIVITIES ?

1 How did the methods of the opponents of the boycott help King and his followers?
2 Construct a mind map to show the methods used by King in the boycott.
3 Write a newspaper article in support of the boycott.
4 Study Source I. Which words in the source show King's Christian approach to his opponents?

Practice question

Give two things you can infer from Source H about the methods used by Martin Luther King. (*For guidance, see page 79.*)

3.2 The success and importance of the Montgomery Bus Boycott

The boycott had shown that unity and solidarity could win, and victory offered hope to those who were fighting for improved civil rights. The NAACP was successful in making a legal case during the boycott and used the *Brown v Topeka* case (see page 10) as a precedent. Moreover, the boycott demonstrated the benefits of a peaceful approach and showed that black Americans were able to organise themselves and above all, show perseverance.

▲ **Source I** Rosa Parks (middle) riding at the front of a bus in 1957, after the end of the boycott

Source J From an interview with James Farmer after the end of the Bus Boycott. Farmer was a civil rights activist and founder of CORE.

The Montgomery Bus Boycott had the charisma to capture the imagination of people. King had a combination of qualities: he was a Southern Baptist preacher, speaking with a Southern accent – that was important – who could preach. At the same time, he could address a Harvard audience and do it intelligently. How many preachers at that time – 1955, 1956 – knew of Gandhi and his work and could speak of non-violence? King was just perfect.

Practice questions

1 Give two things you can infer from Source J about Martin Luther King. (*For guidance, see page 79.*)
2 How useful are Sources I and J for an enquiry into the success of the Montgomery Bus Boycott? Explain your answer, using Sources I and J and your knowledge of the historical context. (*For guidance, see pages 71–73.*)

ACTIVITY **?**

Why was Source I published? Use details from the photograph and your own knowledge to explain your answer.

3.3 The significance of Martin Luther King and the setting up of the SCLC

King was the son of a Baptist minister and grew up in a comfortable middle-class home in Atlanta, Georgia. As a teenager he spoke in his father's church and demonstrated that he had a gift for public oratory. However, he had experienced racial prejudice as a student in such places as Philadelphia, New Jersey and Boston.

MARTIN LUTHER KING JR, 1929–68

1929	Born 15 January
1951	Graduated from Crozer Theological College with a degree in theology
1953	Married Coretta Scott
1955	Completed PhD from Boston University
1955	Led Montgomery Bus Boycott
1957	Formed and led Southern Christian Leadership Conference
1963	'I have a dream' speech. Voted 'Man of the year' by *TIME* magazine
1964	Winner of the Nobel Peace Prize
1968	4 April, assassinated in Memphis

Leader of the boycott

King had been minister at the Dexter Avenue Baptist Church, Montgomery, for less than a year when the bus boycott began. He was chosen as leader of the MIA because of this – he had not been there long enough to grow too close to any particular local organisation. During the dispute he helped to organise the carpools, and when he was prevented from taking out local insurance for the vehicles, he went as far as using Lloyd's of London. His energy and enthusiasm were unbounded in the Montgomery Bus Boycott, and he had the ability to inspire those who worked with him. His idea of using non-violent tactics was similar to the ideas of Gandhi in India, and soon there were many civil rights activists keen to follow King in the quest for equality.

His devout religious beliefs and unwavering faith won him many supporters. He was never intimidated – even when his house was firebombed (see page 17). King received many hate letters each day during the boycott, and some of them threatened his life.

The boycott brought King's philosophy to the fore and gave the movement a clear moral framework. Success also encouraged King to consider further action that would confront inequality and bring about more change.

> **Source K From a comment made by King at the end of the boycott**
>
> We have gained a new sense of dignity and destiny. We have discovered a new and powerful weapon – non-violent resistance.

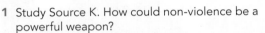

ACTIVITIES

1 Study Source K. How could non-violence be a powerful weapon?
2 Why did King wish to ensure that white Americans were not threatened by the SCLC?
3 Why was securing the vote important for King and his followers?

The setting up of the Southern Christian Leadership Conference

Despite legislation and the raised profile of the civil rights movement, Martin Luther King sought to push for further change. He helped found the Southern Christian Leadership Conference (SCLC) in January 1957, following the Montgomery Bus Boycott. The SCLC was black-led and black-run. It encouraged black Americans to 'seek justice and reject all injustice'. In addition, it promoted King's philosophy of non-violence regardless of the provocation. The SCLC encouraged white Americans to help their fellow black citizens to challenge racism. The SCLC's motto was 'not one hair of one head of one white person shall be harmed'.

Shortly after its establishment the SCLC organised a pilgrimage called the 'Crusade for Citizenship', which marched to the Lincoln Memorial in Washington, DC, in 1958. It also aimed to increase the number of black voters and hoped to force President Eisenhower to speak out on civil rights. The march failed to attract widespread support and Eisenhower refused to be drawn into the debate over civil rights.

3.4 The 1957 Civil Rights Act

Following the successes of the mid-1950s, Congress passed a Civil Rights Act in September 1957, the first for 82 years (Source L). It was evidence of a mood that some changes in society had to be made, albeit gradually. The Act had the support of President Eisenhower, who had always stated that it was impossible to change people's minds by introducing laws. It was hoped that the Act would increase the number of black American voters.

The Act did not win the full support of many Southern Democrats Party members and their opposition led to the watering-down of the contents. Indeed, many black Americans were against the Act because it did not go far enough. However, some thought that it would be the foundation for more wide-reaching acts in the future.

The Civil Rights Act 1957:

- established the US Commission on Civil Rights. Its first project was to look for evidence of racial discrimination in voting rights in Montgomery, Alabama
- emphasised the right of all people to vote, regardless of colour or race
- allowed the Federal Government to intervene if individuals were prevented from voting
- stated that all people had the right to serve on juries.

A second civil rights act was passed in 1960. It renewed the Commission on Civil Rights and stated that people would be prosecuted if they obstructed someone's attempt to register to vote or someone's attempt to actually vote.

> **ACTIVITY** **?**
>
> Why was the 1957 Civil Rights Act important for African Americans?

◀ **Source L** Eisenhower signing the Civil Rights Act of 1957

3.5 How interpretations differ

This section provides guidance on how to answer the question in the exam that asks how two interpretations differ.

Question

Study Interpretations 1 and 2. They give different views about the causes of the urban riots of the 1960s. What is the main difference between the views? Explain your answer, using details from both interpretations.

Interpretation 1 From *Our Changing World: Modern World History From 1919*, Michael Scott-Baumann and David Platt, published in 1989

Many African Americans refused to accept Martin Luther King's call for non-violence. They did not want to seek white support. ... The anger and frustration of urban African Americans erupted in riots. These often started with incidents involving the police. Tempers flared. Punches were thrown, rumours spread and knives were drawn. One such riot broke out in Watts, Los Angeles in 1965.

Interpretation 2: From *The Modern World 1914–80*, P. Sauvain, published in 1989

Progress did not come fast enough for many militant African Americans, oppressed by the poverty of the slums and often unemployed. They resented the failure of many states to implement the civil rights laws and obey the rulings of the Supreme Court. 'We want Black Power', they said. Between 1965 and 1968 there were serious riots in the African American suburbs of over 100 US cities.

How to answer

You are being asked to explain the main difference in the views each interpretation has about the urban riots of the 1960s.

Step 1
You will need to identify the main view that Interpretation 1 has about the causes of the urban riots.

Example
Interpretation 1 is suggesting that the African Americans did not accept King's methods or aims of integration.

Step 2
You will need evidence from Interpretation 1 to support this view.

Example
The interpretation suggests that the African Americans were prepared to use violence by fighting and using knives.

Step 3
You will need to identify the main view that Interpretation 2 has about the causes of urban riots. Use the phrase 'on the other hand' to show that this interpretation gives a different view.

Example
On the other hand, Interpretation 2 is suggesting that the riots began because of oppression and failure of the laws.

Step 4
You will need evidence from Interpretation 2 to support this view.

Example
I know this because the interpretation says that there were riots because the laws were not followed and the Supreme Court's decisions were ignored.

ACTIVITY
Try explaining the main difference between the different views yourself.

4 Opposition to the civil rights movement

African Americans experienced hatred and discrimination, even after emancipation in 1863. In addition, they faced violence and terror from organised groups during this period. The Ku Klux Klan had been an organisation notorious for striking fear and violence into the African American community in and around the 1860s. After declining in popularity at the end of the century, there was a resurgence of interest in the early twentieth century. The Klan grew in numbers and influence in the mid-1920s and experienced another revival in the 1950s as the civil rights movement began. In addition to the terror of the Klan, African Americans experienced other kinds of violence, the worst of which was lynching. More than 2,000 people were lynched in the years 1865–1955 and though there was horror expressed each time one happened, little was done to prosecute the perpetrators. Despite the progress made in the 1950s, there was much opposition to increased African American rights across a range of areas, including within Congress (both in the Senate and House of Representatives), state and local governments and racist organisations.

4.1 The Ku Klux Klan

The **Ku Klux Klan** members were WASPs. They identified themselves as **W**hite, **A**nglo-**S**axon, **P**rotestants, and they saw themselves as being superior to other races, especially African Americans. They were also anti-communist, anti-Jew, anti-Catholic and against all foreigners.

Klansmen dressed in white sheets and wore white hoods. This outfit was designed to conceal the identity of Klan members, who often attacked their victims at night. The white colour symbolised white supremacy. Members carried American flags and lit burning crosses at their night-time meetings. Their leader was known as the Imperial Wizard. Officers of the Klan were known as Klaliffs, Kluds or Klabees.

Members of the Klan carried out lynchings of black people and they beat up and mutilated anyone they considered to be their enemy. They stripped some of their victims and put tar and feathers on their bodies.

Many politicians in the South knew that if they spoke out against the Klan, they would lose votes and might not be elected to Congress. The power of the Klan was still evident in 1946, when 15,000 people marched to the Lincoln Memorial in Washington, DC to demand the organisation be made illegal. As the civil rights movement grew in the 1950s, so did the terror activities of the Klan.

▲ **Source A** Young children with the Grand Dragon of the Klan, near Atlanta, 1948

ACTIVITIES ?

1 Why did the Klan wear such uniforms and have titles such as Klaliffs?
2 What can you learn from Source A about the Klan?

The murder of Emmett Till

In August 1955, Emmett Till, a 14-year old African-American boy from Chicago, visited relatives in the town of Money, Mississippi (see Source B). He was accused of harassing a white woman in a shop – she later claimed that he had taken hold of her by the waist, asked her for a date and when he left the shop he said 'Bye baby' and wolf-whistled at her.

A few days later, the husband and brother-in-law of the woman abducted Till from his relatives' house. They beat and killed Emmett and threw his body into a local river. When the body was found some days later, Till could only be identified by the initials of a ring that he wore. The two men were arrested and identified in court as the men who had abducted Emmett. The trial began in September and lasted four days. The jury's decision took only one hour and one juror said it would have taken less but for the delay of having refreshments taken in to them. The all-white jury found the two white defendants not guilty, explaining that they believed the state had failed to prove the identity of the body.

Till's body was returned to Chicago and his mother ensured that the coffin was open so that people could see the extent of the beating that Emmett had taken. She hoped to shame the authorities in Mississippi and also show the kind of atrocities African Americans endured. Many African Americans were appalled by the manner of Till's death and became involved in the civil rights movement as a result. Indeed, it had a similar effect on many white Americans.

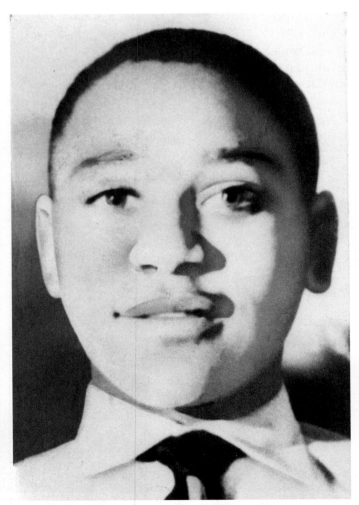

▲ **Source B** Emmett Till, the fourteen-year-old African American who was abducted and murdered

Source C Part of an article from the *Chicago Defender*, a weekly newspaper for African-American readers. The article was published shortly after the death of Emmett Till

How long must we wait for the Federal Government to act? Whenever a crisis arises involving our lives or our rights we look to Washington hopefully for help. It seldom comes.

In the current case, the Department of Justice hastily issued a statement declaring that it was making a thorough investigation to determine if young Till's civil rights had been violated. The Department evidently concluded that the kidnapping and lynching of an African American boy in Mississippi are not violations of his rights. The trial is over, and this miscarriage of justice must not be left unavenged.

At this point we can only conclude that the administration and the Justice Department have decided to uphold the way of life of Mississippi and the South.

ACTIVITIES ?

1 Write a headline of about six words for the Chicago Defender about the death of Emmett Till.

2 Study Source C.
   a) What is a 'miscarriage of justice'?
   b) How useful is Source B as evidence of the reaction to Emmett Till's death?

Practice question

Explain why the death of Emmett Till was important in the civil rights movement.

You may use the following in your answer:
- Differences between the North and South
- Publicity for civil rights

You **must** also use information of your own.

(For guidance, see pages 94–95.)

4.2 Opposition to desegregation in the South

Following the *Brown v Topeka* decision (see page 10), opposition from white Americans to improved civil rights in the South grew quickly.

White Citizens' Councils

White Citizens' Councils were set up to fight the *Brown v Topeka* decision and they campaigned against the NAACP (see page 9) which had fought strongly in the *Brown v Topeka* case. Some Councils tried to distance themselves from the violence of the Ku Klux Klan, though some were open to its use. The Councils also tried to prevent African Americans from registering to vote. The Councils held mass rallies in order to recruit new members and shape public opinion (see Source D).

During the Bus Boycott, the White Citizens' Councils tried to stop the boycott by pressuring insurance agencies throughout the South to cancel policies for church-owned vehicles. Furthermore, Martin Luther King was concerned that the activities of the Councils would deter white Americans from supporting the African American cause. King accused the Councils of being 'ungodly, unethical, un-Christian and un-American' and could not understand why the Federal Government did not criticise the Councils for their activities. In June 1963, Medgar Evers (see page 39) was killed by a member of a White Citizens' Council.

▲ **Source D** A White Citizens' Council Meeting, New Orleans, 1960

Source E From S. D. Cook (an African American Professor of Politics), *Political Movements and Organisations*, published in 1964

White Citizens' Councils, employing the powerful weapons of economic reprisal, political pressure, psychological and emotional terror sought to frighten and to silence not only African Americans but also liberal whites as well and to keep them from participating in desegregation activities.

Source F From the inauguration speech of Governor John Patterson of Alabama, January 1959

... white and black children should have access to equal school facilities but they must be segregated. I will oppose with every ounce of energy I possess and will use every power at my command to prevent any mixing of races in the classrooms of this state ... any attempt to integrate schools of this state by force would cause turmoil, violence and chaos ...

ACTIVITIES

1 How useful are Sources D and F as evidence of opposition to desegregation in the South in the 1950s?
2 Study Source E. Why did White Citizens' Councils want to keep whites from participating in desegregation activities?

Practice question

Give two things you can infer from Source D about White Citizens' Councils. *(For guidance, see page 79.)*

4.3 Congress and the 'Dixiecrats'

Progress towards improved civil rights also met opposition within Congress. In 1956 19 **senators** and 77 members of the House of Representatives signed the **Southern Manifesto**. This document condemned the Brown decision and called it 'a clear abuse of judicial power'. The Manifesto also stated: 'The original Constitution does not mention education. Neither does any other amendment. The debates … clearly show that there was no intent that it should affect the systems of education maintained by the states.' The Manifesto encouraged states to resist carrying any changes to **segregation** and stressed that if changes were made by the Federal Government, then the white public would not accept them and there would be an explosion of hate in the future. However, this was scaremongering from the politicians.

Thus the Southern politicians were trying to use the Constitution to support segregation and also accuse the Federal Government of interfering with individual states' running of education. Southern state legislatures continued to pass laws and resolutions aimed at preventing the Brown decision and in 1956, the Virginia state legislature passed one resistance measure that cut off all state aid to desegregated schools.

Despite opposition in Congress to changes to civil rights, two Acts were passed in 1957 and 1960. Both Acts were introduced to protect the voting rights of American citizens and led to the Voting Rights Act of 1965 (see page 48).

The 'Dixiecrats'

The term 'Dixiecrat' eventually became used to describe white southern **Democrats** opposed to civil rights legislation. The issue of civil rights had split the Democrats in the 1948 presidential election. Truman was acutely aware of the racial tensions within the USA, but he knew that he would have to tread carefully because many of the so-called **Dixiecrats** (Southern Democrat Party politicians) would vote against any of his reforming measures. He wanted to introduce a civil rights bill, and also put forward an anti-lynching bill, but both were rejected by the southern Dixiecrats. They even formed their own political party and won more than one million votes in the 1948 presidential election. The Dixiecrats wanted to continue segregation and did not want any interference from the Federal Government when decisions about race had to be made.

In the 1950s, although the Dixiecrats did not continue as a party, they continued to oppose changes in civil rights. In 1957, Senator Thurmond (see Source G) of South Carolina, a Dixiecrat, conducted the longest ever **filibuster** (24 hours and 18 minutes nonstop) in an attempt to prevent the passage of the Civil Rights Bill.

▼ **Source G** Senator Strom Thurmond, a Dixiecrat, who strongly opposed progress in civil rights for African Americans

Many Dixiecrats joined White Citizens' Councils (see page 25) in order to continue their struggle. Some even left the Democrat Party and joined the **Republicans**. In the 1960 Presidential election, John Kennedy had to be careful not to upset the Dixiecrats and their supporters for fear of losing their votes. He did this by keeping the issue of civil rights low on his agenda and focusing more on discussing foreign affairs.

ACTIVITIES ?

1 How did the term 'Dixiecrat' emerge?
2 Suggest reasons why the Southern politicians used the Constitutions of the States to support their policy of segregation.
3 Conduct your own research on Senator Thurmond. Write a brief summary of his political career – about 150 words.

Protest, progress and radicalism 1960–75

This key topic examines the key developments in the civil rights movement from 1960 to 1975. The chapters cover vital issues such as sit-ins, Freedom Rides, the peace marches, the Civil Rights Act, Malcolm X, Black Power, the death of King and an assessment of the progress made by African Americans.

Each chapter within this key topic explains a key issue and examines important lines of enquiry, as outlined below.

CHAPTER 5 PROGRESS, 1960–62

- The significance of Greensboro and the sit-in movement.
- The Freedom Riders. Ku Klux Klan violence and the Anniston bomb.
- The James Meredith case, 1962.

CHAPTER 6 PEACEFUL PROTESTS AND THEIR IMPACT, 1963–65

- King and the peace marches of 1963 in Birmingham, Alabama, and Washington. Freedom Summer and the Mississippi murders.
- The roles of President Kennedy and Johnson and the passage of the Civil Rights Act 1964.
- Selma and the Voting Rights Act 1965.

CHAPTER 7 MALCOLM X AND BLACK POWER, 1963–70

- Malcolm X, his beliefs, methods and involvement with the Black Muslims. His later change of attitude and assassination.
- Reasons for the emergence of Black Power. The significance of Stokely Carmichael and the 1968 Mexico Olympics.
- The methods and achievements of the Black Panther movement.

CHAPTER 8 THE CIVIL RIGHTS MOVEMENT, 1965–75

- The riots of 1965–67 and the Kerner Report, 1968.
- King's campaign in the North. The assassination of Martin Luther King and its impact.
- The extent of progress in civil rights by 1975.

TIMELINE 1960–75

1960 February	Greensboro sit-in	1964 June	Mississippi murders
1961 May	First Freedom Ride	1964 July	Civil Rights Act passed
1961 May	Anniston bomb attack	1965 February	Assassination of Malcolm X
1962 April	Voter Education Project set up	1965 August	Voting Rights Act passed
1962 June	James Meredith case begins	1968 February	Kerner Report published
1963 June	Medgar Evers shot	1968 April	Assassination of Martin Luther King
1963 August	Birmingham march	1968 October	Protest at the Mexico Olympics
1964 June	Freedom Summer		

The civil rights movement continued to make progress in the early 1960s due the publicity provided by new methods adopted by activists for the movement. These new methods included the 'sit-in' movement which originated in Greensboro, North Carolina, as well as the emergence of the Freedom Riders whose activities challenged the continued illegal segregation of public transport in the South. Moreover, the issue of black education, this time at university level, made front page news as a result of the James Meredith case. Further publicity was provided by the Albany Movement which campaigned for black voting rights.

5.1 Greensboro and the sit-in movement

During the late 1950s there were many instances of sit-ins, sit-down demonstrations and boycotts (see Figure 5.1). These were eventually given the term 'direct action'. The black activist leaders soon realised that direct action often resulted in white violence, which tended to lose support for the whites. The event that pushed the civil rights movement into greater activity came not from organisations like CORE or the NAACP, however, but from students at a college in North Carolina.

The Greensboro sit-in

Just as King was emerging as a powerful force in the civil rights movement, events in North Carolina showed the lengths to which students would go to fight segregation. A sit-in was held at the Greensboro branch of Woolworths – four black students from a local college demanded to be served at a whites-only lunch counter and, on being refused, remained seated at the counter until the shop closed (see Source A). The next day, they were accompanied by 27 more students and the day after a further 80 joined them. By the fifth day there were 300. The shop agreed to make a few concessions, but the students later resumed their protests and some were arrested for trespass. The students then boycotted any shop in Greensboro that had segregated lunch counters. Sales immediately dropped and eventually segregation ended. During the sit-ins the students had to endure violence and assaults, but they were careful not to retaliate, copying the peaceful tactics Martin Luther King had used at Montgomery. For the second time, a non-violent approach that hit the local economy through boycotts was used successfully. King visited Greensboro at the height of the sit-in and promised the support of the SCLC.

Sit-ins very quickly became a tool of protest, especially in cities where there were many students and in places where African American adults had made some progress in civil rights.

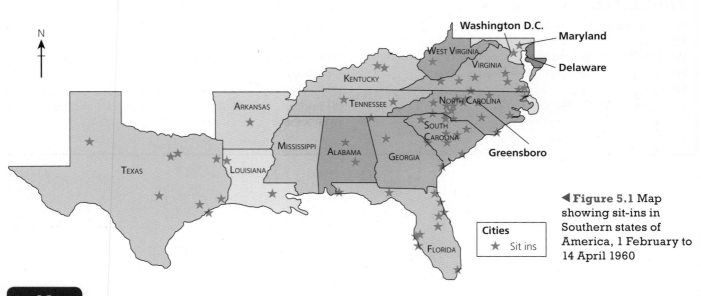

◄ Figure 5.1 Map showing sit-ins in Southern states of America, 1 February to 14 April 1960

▲ **Source A** Greensboro students at the Woolworths counter, 2 February 1960

Student Non-violent Co-ordinating Committee (SNCC)

The SNCC was founded at Shaw University in Raleigh, North Carolina, in April 1960. It received a grant of $800 from the SCLC to help establish itself. Its first chairman was Nashville college student and political activist Marion Barry. The SNCC, or 'Snick' as it became known, continued its efforts to desegregate lunch counters through non-violent confrontations, but it had only modest success. In May 1961, the group expanded its focus to support local efforts in voter registration as well as public accommodations desegregation. It played a major role in the key events of the early 1960s, including sit-ins, Freedom Rides, the march on Washington (see page 40) and the 'Freedom Summer' (see page 42).

ACTIVITIES

1 What is meant by the term 'direct action'?

2 Conduct your own research into CORE, NAACP, SCLC and SNCC. Try to find out five additional points about each organisation. (Use the internet, reference books and refer also to individuals such as Martin Luther King and Marion Barry.)

3 Why were the events at Greensboro so important for the civil rights movement?

4 Prepare a one-minute talk to explain why you support the method of the sit-in.

5 What is paradoxical about Source A? Explain your answer carefully.

6 What can you learn from Source B about the SNCC?

Practice question

Give two things you can infer from Source B about the SNCC. (For guidance, see page 79.)

▲ **Source B** Badges worn by SNCC members in the 1960s. The badge on the right was the Alabama Christian Movement for Human Rights

5.2 The Freedom Riders

In December 1960, the Supreme Court decided that all bus stations and terminals that served interstate travellers should be integrated. The Congress of Racial Equality (CORE) wanted to test that decision by employing the tactic of the Freedom Ride. CORE had declined in importance and influence since the late 1950s, and was seeking to revive itself. If there was continued failure to carry out the laws passed to ensure integration, CORE would be able to show that narrow-mindedness and racism still existed in the Southern states.

The first of the Freedom Rides began in May 1961, when James Farmer – the National Director of CORE – and twelve volunteers left Washington DC by bus to travel to New Orleans (see Figure 5.2). There was little trouble on the first part of the journey, even when the black Americans used whites-only facilities to ensure integration was taking place. However, things changed once the freedom riders got to Alabama.

The Anniston bomb

In Alabama, one of the buses being ridden by the Freedom Riders was firebombed outside Anniston, on Mothers' Day – Sunday 14 May 1961. As the bus burned, the mob held the doors shut, intent on burning the riders to death. An exploding fuel tank caused the mob to retreat, allowing the riders to escape the bus, but they were viciously beaten by men armed with clubs, bricks, iron pipes and knives as they tried to flee. Warning shots fired into the air by highway patrolmen prevented the riders from being lynched on the spot.

When the Freedom Riders reached Birmingham later that day, there was no protection for them and they were attacked by an angry mob – the police chief, Eugene 'Bull' Connor, had given most of the police the day off. These events forced the new president, John F. Kennedy, to intervene, and he secured a promise from the state **senator** in Jackson that there would be no further mob violence. However, when the riders arrived in Jackson, they were immediately arrested when they tried to use the whites-only waiting room.

The riders continue

In Montgomery, white racists beat up several of the Freedom Riders. In Jackson, Mississippi, 27 freedom riders from the SNCC and SCLC were jailed for 67 days for sitting in the whites-only section of the bus station. During that year, the membership of CORE doubled, reaching 52,000 by December 1961. The riders continued throughout the summer, and more than 300 of them were imprisoned in Jackson alone.

Source C From an interview with James Peck, who rode the first Freedom bus. Here he is describing what happened when he arrived in Anniston in May 1961

As Charles Person and I entered the white waiting room and approached the lunch counter, we were grabbed and pushed outside into an alleyway. As soon as we got into the alleyway and were out of sight of the onlookers in the waiting room, six men started swinging at me with fists and pipes. Five others attacked Charles. Within seconds, I was unconscious.

Source E From an interview with James Zwerg in 1999. Zwerg was talking about his involvement in the freedom rides

Usually, a white man got picked out for the violence first.... I remember being kicked in the spine and hearing my back crack... I fell on my back and a foot came down on my face. The next thing I remember is waking up in the back of a vehicle... I passed out again and when I woke up I was in another moving vehicle with some very southern sounding whites.... A white nurse told me that another little crowd were going to try and lynch me. They had come within a half block of the hospital. She said that she knocked me out in case they did make it, so that I would not be aware of what was happening.

▲ **Source D** The burnt-out bus at Anniston, May 1961

▲ **Source F** John Lewis (left) and James Zwerg – two Freedom Riders beaten up by a white mob in Montgomery, Alabama, May 1961

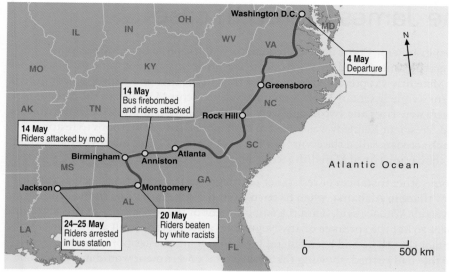

◄ **Figure 5.2** Map of the Freedom Rides, 1961

Ku Klux Klan violence

Attacks on the Freedom Riders by the **Ku Klux Klan** increased. In 1983, certain FBI documents were handed over to the US Justice Department which revealed that the FBI was aware of the Ku Klux Klan's plans to attack the freedom riders in Birmingham. Moreover, the documents show that one Birmingham police officer told the Klan that no matter how viciously the Freedom Riders were attacked, there would be no arrests.

Government reaction

The **Attorney General**, Robert Kennedy (see page 34), did not wish to see the situation escalate and was hoping that he would not have to send in US marshals to enforce the law. Violence was avoided in Mississippi when it became clear that marshals would be used. On 22 September, the Interstate Commerce Commission issued a regulation that: 'prohibited carriers of interstate passengers from having anything whatsoever to do with any terminal facilities which are so operated, arranged, or maintained so as to involve any separation on the basis of race, color, creed or national origin.'

The Freedom Rides had been successful. By the early 1960s, more and more young white people were protesting against racial discrimination. They pointed out that the American claim to have a democracy was a contradiction and that the USA's way of life was based on the oppression of black Americans (see Source G).

The Freedom Rides of the early 1960s once again raised awareness of the civil rights campaign. The rides were seen across the USA and the publicity gained was invaluable to those in the civil rights movement. The next event in the path to civil rights was crucial, because it involved not only education, but the new president, John F. Kennedy. Kennedy had narrowly won the presidential election of 1960 and the

votes of African Americans was a contributory factor in his success. There was an expectation therefore that he would support the demand for civil rights.

> **Source G** From V. Harding, *The Other American Revolution*, published in 1980
>
> These young people were believers. When they sang in jail, in mass meetings, in front of police and state troopers 'We shall overcome', they meant it ... overcoming meant 'freedom' and 'rights' and 'justice' and black and white together ... But they knew they were part of a revolution and they believed that if they persisted ... they would make it.

ACTIVITIES

1 Prepare a statement for a local television station to explain why the Freedom Riders will pass through that area.

2 Why was the Anniston bomb so important?

3 Study Source E. What can you learn from Source E about the attitudes of white people during the Freedom Rides?

4 What can you learn from Source G about changes in the civil rights movement?

Practice questions

1 Give two things you can infer from Source C (page 30) about the Freedom Riders. *(For guidance, see page 79.)*

2 How useful are Sources C and E (page 30) for an enquiry into the Freedom Rides? Explain your answer using Sources C and E and your knowledge of the historical context. *(For guidance, see pages 71–73.)*

5.3 The James Meredith case

In June 1962, the Supreme Court upheld a federal court decision to force Mississippi University to accept James Meredith as a student. The university did not want any black students and Meredith was prevented from registering. In his first major involvement in civil rights, President Kennedy sent in 320 federal marshals to escort Meredith to the campus (see Source H). There were riots and two people were killed, 166 marshals and 210 demonstrators were wounded. President Kennedy was forced to send more than 2,000 troops to restore order. The black activists called the event 'The Battle of Oxford'. Three hundred soldiers had to remain on the campus until Meredith received his degree three years later.

There were some other instances of resistance to integration in education, such as that led by Governor Wallace in Alabama, when he tried to stop black Americans from enrolling at the state university. Wallace said, 'I am the embodiment of the sovereignty of this state, and I will be present to bar the entrance of any Negro who attempts to enroll at the university.' However, the fact that there had been federal intervention at Mississippi University indicated the tide had turned, showing that the Federal government would now intervene when there was resistance to integration in education.

▲ **Source H** African American student James Meredith being escorted across the University of Mississippi campus by US marshals, October 1962

> **Source I** Part of Bob Dylan's song 'Oxford Town'. Dylan was singing about the James Meredith case. Oxford was the site of Mississippi University
>
> He went down to Oxford Town
>
> Guns and clubs followed him down
>
> All because his face was brown
>
> Better get away from Oxford Town
>
> Oxford Town around the bend
>
> He come in to the door, he couldn't get in
>
> All because of the color of his skin
>
> What do you think about that, my frien'?
>
> Oxford Town in the afternoon
>
> Ev'rybody singin' a sorrowful tune
>
> Two men died 'neath the Mississippi moon
>
> Somebody better investigate soon
>
> Oxford Town, Oxford Town
>
> Ev'rybody's got their heads bowed down
>
> The sun don't shine above the ground
>
> Ain't a-goin' down to Oxford Town

ACTIVITIES

1 What can you learn about the Meredith case from Source H?
2 Study Source I. Why do you think this song became popular with many people in the USA?
3 Why was the Meredith case important for civil rights?

Practice questions

1 Give two things you can infer from Source I about the Meredith case. (*For guidance, see page 79.*)
2 How useful are Sources H and I for an enquiry into the Meredith case? Explain your answer, using Sources H and I and your knowledge of the historical context. (*For guidance, see pages 71–73.*)

5.4 What progress had been made by 1962?

In spite of legislation and limited progress, African Americans could not expect immediate changes. Indeed, there was still outright opposition to change and once again, direct action was taken by activists. This time, the scene moved to Albany, Georgia, where it was decided that there would be an all-out attempt to de-segregate a whole community.

The Albany Movement, 1961–62

In late 1961, several hundred Freedom Riders were arrested in Albany, Georgia. Following this, various black groups created the Albany Movement to oppose segregation in the town. Hundreds of activists went to Albany and their work induced Martin Luther King to visit. He was arrested following a march; he spent a short time in jail because he refused to pay the fine. Despite a concerted effort, the meetings, marches and demonstrations failed to end segregation. Albany's parks and swimming pools were closed, and schools continued to be segregated despite the *Brown v Topeka* case and Little Rock. One success was a small increase in the numbers of black Americans who registered to vote, but many in the civil rights movement saw the events at Albany as a failure.

> **ACTIVITY** ?
>
> What can you learn from Sources J and K about events at Albany?

◄ **Source J** Protesters demonstrating in Albany during the effort to desegregate the city, 1962

◄ **Source K** Protestors praying following their arrest for parading without a permit, Albany 1962

33

The Voter Education Project

The Freedom Rides caused Robert Kennedy to fear violent confrontations between the black civil rights groups and white segregationists. He felt that if more black Americans voted then they would be able to have a greater say in such issues as housing and education. Kennedy met various groups, and the Voter Education Project was set up in 1962.

The project was staffed mainly by members of the SNCC (see page 29) and they spent much time with eligible voters, showing them how to register and overcome the barriers that were placed in front of them.

The project resulted in more than 650,000 new registrations, but many people were still refused the right to vote on dubious grounds. SNCC workers were subject to harassment. For example, in Georgia, several churches were bombed, workers were beaten up and some were even shot. Those who did register and voted were sometimes evicted from their land, sacked from their jobs and refused credit. SNCC members felt betrayed because they thought Kennedy would protect them – both President Kennedy and Robert Kennedy were of the opinion that the local police should protect the SNCC workers from the Ku Klux Klan and White Citizens' Councils, but in many cases this did not happen. In New Orleans, White Citizens' Councils (see page 25) actually bought one-way tickets for black Americans who wished to leave the segregated South and move north.

"BY TH' WAY, WHAT'S THAT BIG WORD?"

Source L A cartoon in a US newspaper, 1964. The caption was: 'By the way, what's that big word?'

◀ **Source M** A poster from the Voter Education Project encouraging African Americans to vote

Mixed progress

By the end of 1962, some progress had been made in the campaign for civil rights, but there was still entrenched racism in the South. Moreover, the various civil rights groups had not always agreed among themselves about the best way to proceed. Although Martin Luther King was undoubtedly the leading figure, not enough had been done to raise the issue of civil rights to the top of the domestic agenda in the USA. All this changed in 1963.

ACTIVITIES

1 Copy and complete the table below, explaining the reasons why each was successful/unsuccessful.

	Successful	Unsuccessful
Freedom Rides		
The Albany Project		
The Voter Education Project		

3 Study Source L. What message is this cartoon trying to put across?

2 Study Source M. Why did the Voter Education Project use such posters in its work?

Practice question

Explain why the civil rights movement made progress in the years 1960-62.

You may use the following in your answer:
- The sit-ins
- James Meredith case

You **must** also use information of your own.

(For guidance, see pages 94–95.)

5.5 Why the interpretations differ

This section provides guidance on how to answer the question which asks you to suggest one reason why the interpretations give different views. Look at the question below. Then read the guidance on how to answer on page 37.

Question

Suggest one reason why Interpretations 1 and 2 give different views about the causes of the urban riots of the 1960s. You may use the sources to help explain your answer.

Interpretation 1 From *Our Changing World: Modern World History From 1919*, Michael Scott-Baumann and David Platt, published in 1989

Many African Americans refused to accept Martin Luther King's call for non-violence. They did not want to seek white support. … The anger and frustration of urban African Americans erupted in riots. These often started with incidents involving the police. Tempers flared. Punches were thrown, rumours spread and knives were drawn. One such riot broke out in Watts, Los Angeles in 1965.

Interpretation 2 From *The Modern World 1914–80*, P. Sauvain, published in 1989

Progress did not come fast enough for many militant African Americans, oppressed by the poverty of the slums and often unemployed. They resented the failure of many states to implement the Civil Rights laws and obey the rulings of the Supreme Court. 'We want Black Power' they said. Between 1965 and 1968 there were serious riots in the African American suburbs of over 100 US cities.

Source A Part of the Black Panther Party Manifesto, October 1966

2. We want full employment for our people.

We believe that the Federal Government is responsible and obligated to give every man employment or a guaranteed income. We believe that if the white American businessmen will not give full employment, then the means of production should be taken from the businessmen and placed in the community so that the people of the community can organize and employ all of its people and give a high standard of living.

4. We want decent housing, fit for the shelter of human beings.

We believe that if the white landlords will not give decent housing to our black community, then the housing and the land should be made into cooperatives so that our community, with government aid, can build and make decent housing for its people.

Source B From Stokely Carmichael, *New York Review of Books*, 22 September 1966

In a sense, I blame ourselves – together with the mass media – for what has happened in the riots in Watts, Harlem, Chicago, Cleveland, Omaha. Each time the people in those cities saw Martin Luther King get slapped, they became angry; when they saw four little black girls bombed to death, they were angrier; and when nothing happened, they were steaming. We had nothing to offer that they could see, except to go out and be beaten again. We helped to build their frustration.

How to answer

On page 36 you were shown how to explain one difference between these two interpretations. Now you have to give one reason why these interpretations are different. You can use two sources to help you with this answer.

There are three reasons as to why the two interpretations differ. You will only need to give one of these.

First possible reason (remember you only have to explain one of the reasons)

Step 1
The interpretations may differ because they have given weight to two different sources. You need to identify the views given in the two sources.

Example
Source A suggests that Martin Luther King's policy of non-violence only created frustration. Source B suggests that there was unemployment among African Americans.

Step 2
Now you need to show how the sources match the views of the two interpretations and identify the views given in the interpretations that match.

Example
Source A provides some support for Interpretation 2, which stresses that trouble came from unemployment and bad housing. Source B provides some support for Interpretation 1, which suggests that people found the cheek-turning a waste of time.

Second possible reason (remember you only have to explain one of the reasons)

Step 3
The interpretations may differ because they are partial extracts and in this case they do not actually contradict one another.

Example
Both interpretations suggest that there were riots. Interpretation 1 says that it was to do with the African American approach. Interpretation 2 emphasises the failure to follow the law.

Third possible reason (remember you only have to explain one of the reasons)

Step 4
They may differ because the authors have a different emphasis.

Example
Interpretation 1 focuses more on the police action. On the other hand, Interpretation 2 focuses more on the militancy of African Americans.

6 Peaceful protests and their impact, 1963–65

The civil rights issue seemed to explode in 1963. Although the sit-ins had enjoyed some success, there was still no federal law that made Southern states integrate their public facilities. The profile was raised by a number of marches that gained worldwide publicity. It was these marches that brought Martin Luther King to worldwide prominence and led to two crucial pieces of legislation – the Civil Rights Act (1964) and the Voting Rights Act (1965).

6.1 Events in Birmingham, Alabama

In order to avoid desegregating its parks, playgrounds, swimming pools and golf courses, the city of Birmingham, Alabama, simply closed them all. The **Southern Christian Leadership Conference (SCLC)** sought to challenge the city with Project C – 'Confrontation' – which would use the tactics of sit-ins and marches to press for **desegregation** at lunch counters initially. It was hoped that the demonstrations would achieve maximum publicity across the USA. Birmingham had a population of about 350,000, of whom about 150,000 were black Americans. King hoped to mobilise a large number of them in the planned demonstrations.

The demonstrations began on 3 April 1963, and on 6 April some activists were arrested. Police Chief Bull Connor closed all public parks and playgrounds. This prompted King to address a large rally, at which he said it was better to go to jail in dignity rather than just accept **segregation**. King was arrested in a further demonstration on 12 April and jailed for defying a ban on marches. He was arrested on Good Friday and during his short stay in prison, he wrote 'Letter from Birmingham Jail'. This letter became one of the most famous documents of the civil rights movement, and many see it as one of the most powerful in history.

Once again, King explained why African Americans were tired and angry at their humiliating treatment in their own country. He pointed out how the citizens of the new independent countries in Africa and Asia had more rights than African Americans and that progress was excruciatingly slow in the USA.

In the letter, King also wrote how he understood that people were impatient for change. He stressed that many in the USA had no idea of the fears that African Americans had and that these fears began early in life and were felt by all – young, old, male and female. He was keen to point out how the police did little or nothing to stop the hatred and violence and in fact, often committed violence themselves against African Americans. Most importantly, King pointed out the fact that there was tremendous poverty among African Americans in a country of incredible wealth.

ACTIVITY

Work in pairs. Find King's 'Letter from Birmingham Jail' on the Martin Luther King Center website. Choose what you consider to be the ten most important points of the letter and prepare a presentation for the class.

Events worsen

The situation worsened on King's release from jail on 20 April. It was decided that children and students would be used in the demonstrations, and this seemed to change the methods used by the police. On 3 May, Police Chief Connor allowed his men to set dogs on the protesters (see Source A), and then called in the fire department to use powerful water hoses (see Source C). Connor placed almost 2,000 demonstrators in jail. Around 1,300 children were arrested and there was concern about students missing school. Television crews captured the events, and these images were seen not only across the USA but all over the world. Photographs of the demonstration and police reaction were published in national newspapers. This gave King all the publicity he wanted. It showed the violence of the authorities in the face of peaceful demonstrators. By 3 May there was chaos in Birmingham.

President Kennedy's involvement

It was at this stage that President Kennedy became involved – he sent Assistant **Attorney General** Burke Marshall to mediate between the parties in the hope of finding a solution. Desegregation was eventually introduced in Birmingham. A consequence of the violence was Kennedy's decision to bring in a Civil Rights Bill. He stated that, 'The events in Birmingham … have so increased the cries for equality that no city or state legislative body can prudently choose to ignore them' and that events in Birmingham 'had damaged America'. Talks between King and the Birmingham city leaders brought a settlement by 9 May, and it was agreed that desegregation would take place in the city within 90 days.

On that same day, 11 June 1963, Medgar Evers, leader of the Mississippi National Association for the Advancement of Colored People, was shot dead in Jackson by a white sniper.

> **Source B** From a speech made on television by President Kennedy on 11 June 1963, about the need to improve civil rights for black Americans
>
> We preach freedom around the world, and we mean it … But are we to say to the world – and much more importantly to one another – that this is the land of the free except for the Negroes? We face a moral crisis as a country and a people. It cannot be met by repressive police action. It cannot be left to increased demonstrations in our streets. It is a time to act in Congress and in our daily lives.

ACTIVITIES ?

1. Why did King choose Birmingham to demonstrate?
2. Suggest reasons why President Kennedy became so involved in the crisis at Birmingham.
3. Study Source B. What did President Kennedy mean when he said 'We face a moral crisis'?

Practice questions

1. How useful are Sources A and C for an enquiry into the tactics used by the police in Birmingham in 1963? Explain your answer. (*For guidance, see pages 71–73.*)
2. Give two things you can infer from Source B about Kennedy's attitude to civil rights. (*For guidance, see page 79.*)

▲ **Source A** Police dogs attacking civil rights demonstrators in Birmingham, Alabama, 3 May 1963

▲ **Source C** Fire hoses being turned on demonstrators in Birmingham, 3 May 1963. The hoses were powerful enough to rip the bark off trees, loosen bricks from walls and knock people down

6.2 The march on Washington

After Birmingham, the civil rights groups wanted to maintain their impetus and some sought to commemorate the centenary of the freeing of the slaves in 1863. The idea of a huge march on Washington, DC, was put forward by Philip Randolph, who had suggested a similar march in 1941. Randolph was given close assistance by Bayard Rustin and Cleveland Robinson (see Source D).

The key groups of NAACP, CORE, SNCC and SCLC took part in organising the march. King was keen to have the march because he knew that there were those in the movement who felt that progress was slow and who might drift towards violence if the high profile was not sustained (see page 51). Indeed, the Washington police halted leave for its 3,000 officers and called on the services of 1,000 police officers from neighbouring locations in case there was violence. There were also 2,000 members of the National Guard on standby. President Kennedy also feared violence at the march and he asked the organisers to call it off.

The march initially began as a cry for jobs and freedom, but its aims broadened to cover those of the whole of the civil rights movement. There was naturally a demand for the passage of Kennedy's Civil Rights Bill.

▲ **Source D** Bayard Rustin (left) and Cleveland Robinson, two of the organisers of the march on Washington

The Washington March

When the march took place, there were about 250,000 demonstrators (it has been estimated that there were around 80,000 white supporters) – the organisers had expected less than half this figure. People came from all over the USA – by plane, train, bus and car. When **senators** and **congressmen** were seen, there were chants of 'Pass the bill' (meaning Kennedy's Civil Rights Bill). Before the speakers, Bob Dylan sang several songs, one of which was called 'Only a Pawn in Their Game' and he was joined by other protest singers. Not all the speakers were moderate in their approach. John Lewis of the SNCC was forced to amend his speech, but even so, the one he delivered was very powerful (see Source E).

> **Source E** From John Lewis' speech, Washington, DC, 28 August 1963
>
> We are tired of being beaten by policemen. We are tired of seeing our people locked up in jail over and over again. We march today for jobs and freedom, but we have nothing to be proud of, for hundreds and thousands of our brothers are not here – for they have no money for their transportation, for they are receiving starvation wages … or no wages at all. We must have legislation that will protect the Mississippi sharecroppers, who have been forced to leave their homes because they dared to exercise their right to register to vote.

'I have a dream'

King was the final speaker of the day and his speech has now become part of the lore of the struggle for civil rights. He used his skill as an orator and included many biblical references, which appealed to all sections in society.

In the speech, he quoted from the American Declaration of Independence and looked to a future where he saw racial equality in the USA.

Although there were some detractors – Malcolm X (see page 52) called it a 'farce on Washington' – the march on Washington was hailed as a great success. It was televised across the USA and did much for the civil rights movement. It brought together different sections of US society and put further pressure on President Kennedy to move forward on civil rights.

> **ACTIVITY** ?
>
> Find King's 'I have a dream' speech on the Martin Luther King Center website. Can you suggest reasons why it has become one of the most famous in history?

▲ **Source F** Martin Luther King at the Lincoln Memorial, August 1963

Effects of the Washington March

After the march, King and the other leaders met President Kennedy to discuss civil rights legislation. Kennedy was keen to let them know of his own commitment to the Civil Rights Bill. However, all those at the meeting were aware that there were many **Republican Party** politicians still opposed to any changes. No opposition politician in the **Senate** changed his mind about Kennedy's Civil Rights Bill.

King's hopes seemed illusory because in September 1963, four black girls were killed in a bomb attack while attending Sunday school in Birmingham. Violence erupted on the day of the bombing and two black youths were killed in the aftermath.

ACTIVITIES

1 Study Source D (page 40). What did the organisers mean by the word 'freedom'?

2 Why was it important for the civil rights movement to have the support of famous actors and protest singers?

3 Working in pairs, put forward a list of reasons why the march on Washington was a success.

4 Study Source E (page 40). In what ways is Lewis different to King in his view of civil rights?

5 Can you suggest reasons why King's 'I have a dream' speech has become one of the most famous in history?

Practice question

How useful are Sources E (page 40) and F for an enquiry into the Washington March? Explain your answer using Sources E and F and your knowledge of the historical context. (*For guidance, see pages 71–73.*)

6.3 The Freedom Summer and the Mississippi murders

The civil rights movement seemed to stall in late 1963. Kennedy's Civil Rights Bill (see page 46) went through its first stages in November 1963, but his assassination delayed its progress. After the high point of the Washington march and now the delay in passing the Bill, the civil rights movement organised the Freedom Summer in June 1964. Its aim was to increase the number of registered voters in Mississippi, which had the lowest number of registered voters of blacks in the USA (around seven per cent).

CORE, the SNCC and the NAACP acted together in organising the Freedom Summer, and in doing so came together to form the Mississippi Freedom Party (MFDP). More than 80,000 people joined. They established 30 **Freedom Schools** in towns throughout Mississippi in order to address the racial inequalities in Mississippi's educational system (see Source G). Volunteers from across the USA taught in the schools. The curriculum included black history and the philosophy of the civil rights movement. It has been estimated that more than 3,000 students attended these schools that summer and almost 70,000 by the end of the year.

The schools and volunteers became the target of white racists, and there were bombings and assaults – sometimes by the police. More than 30 churches were bombed. However, the Freedom Summer became notorious because of the murder of three of the project's volunteers – James Chaney and his two white colleagues, Andrew Goodman and Michael Schwerner.

ACTIVITY ?

Why was Mississippi chosen as the focus of the 1964 Freedom School?

▲ **Source G** Students having a lesson in a Freedom School, Mississippi, 1964

The Mississippi murders

On 21 June 1964, Chaney, Goodman and Schwerner were arrested while they were investigating a church bombing. They were taken in for traffic offences by a policeman who was a member of the **Ku Klux Klan**. They were held for several hours, but were eventually released from police custody. They were never seen again. The police officer had informed his associates in the Klan of the arrests and they began to plan the murders.

Six weeks later, three badly decomposed bodies were discovered under a nearby dam. Goodman and Schwerner had been shot in the chest and Chaney had been severely beaten and shot. (The film *Mississippi Burning*, starring Gene Hackman and Willem Dafoe, is about this incident.) Eventually 18 people were arrested and 7 men were convicted of the murders. None served more than six years in prison.

Reaction to the murders

In the wake of these events the civil rights movement gained support and President Johnson (who came to power following Kennedy's assassination) was firm in his resolve to find the murderers. It was ironic that on 2 July, at the height of this crisis, President Johnson signed the Civil Rights Act (see page 46).

Some of the black members of the Freedom School movement claimed that there was nationwide publicity about the murders only because two of the victims were white. At the end of the Freedom Summer, some activists returned home and turned their attention to different causes. Others, such as Stokely Carmichael (see page 53), began to look at more radical approaches to bringing about change. Nevertheless, most of those involved in the summer's protests saw their actions as successful when, in 1965, the Voting Rights Act was passed (see page 48).

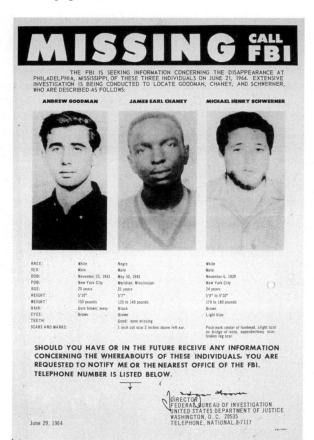

▲ **Source H** An FBI poster raising awareness of the missing Goodman, Chaney and Schwerner, August 1964

ACTIVITIES

1 Study Source H and use your own knowledge. Why was the poster published? Use details from the poster and your own knowledge to explain your answer.

2 What were the results of the 'Freedom Summer'?

Practice question

Give two things you can infer from Source H about the Mississippi murders. (*For guidance, see page 79.*)

6.4 The role of President Kennedy in civil rights

During the 1960 presidential election campaign, Kennedy ensured that he campaigned in urban areas where there were heavy concentrations of black voters. Kennedy was instrumental in securing the release of Martin Luther King from jail in Atlanta in October 1960 after his arrest at a sit-in, an act that won him some support.

When one considers the narrow margin of Kennedy's victory (out of 68 million votes cast, Kennedy won by 112,827 votes), winning the black vote had been crucial. In his inauguration speech, President Kennedy put forward the idea of the New Frontier. One part of this was to achieve equality for black Americans. However, he had to be very astute in his approach because he faced opposition not only from his own party (the Dixiecrats, see page 26) but also white supremacists across the USA.

Kennedy was aware that he had to accept King and his methods. During the Birmingham riots in 1963 (see page 39), Robert Kennedy echoed his brother's views when he said: 'If King loses, worse leaders are going to take his place.'

> **Source I** From a letter from Roy Wilkins, leader of the NAACP, to President John F. Kennedy, January 1961
>
> Dear Mr President, Mrs Wilkins and I were thrilled to be among those who witnessed, in person, your inauguration as 35th President of the United States last Friday. The snow and the cold meant nothing at all after you began your memorable inaugural address.
>
> Please accept our congratulations and our prayers for the accomplishment of all you envision for the good of our country and for the peace of the world.

> **Source J** From a speech by President Kennedy after the University of Alabama was desegregated in 1963
>
> It is as old as the scriptures and is as clear as the American Constitution. The heart of the question is whether all Americans are to be afforded equal rights and equal opportunities, whether we are going to treat our fellow Americans as we want to be treated. If an American, because his skin is dark, cannot eat lunch in a restaurant open to the public, if he cannot send his children to the best school available, if he cannot vote for the public officials who represent him, if, in short, he cannot enjoy the full and free life which all of us want, then who among us would be content to have the color of his skin changed and stand in his place? Who among us would then be content with the counsels of patience and delay?

During his time as president, Kennedy:

- Appointed five black federal judges, including Thurgood Marshall. Marshall was a leading civil rights activist and his appointment showed Kennedy's commitment to this issue.
- Appointed his brother (Robert) as Attorney General. This meant that law courts could be used to ensure that civil rights laws were not circumvented.
- Appointed other black Americans to his administration, such as Carl Rowan (Deputy Assistant Secretary of State), Robert Weaver (Director of the Housing and Home Finance Agency), Mercer Cook (Ambassador to Norway) and George Weaver (Assistant Secretary of Labor).
- Threatened legal action against the state of Louisiana for refusing to fund schools that were not segregated.
- Sent 23,000 government troops to ensure that just one black student, James Meredith, could study at the University of Mississippi (see page 32).
- Threatened to evict the Washington Redskins football team from their stadium, which was funded by the Federal Government, unless they agreed to hire black players.
- Introduced a Civil Rights Bill to Congress in February 1963, which aimed to give black people equality in public housing and education. This decision won him many supporters among black Americans.

However, Kennedy's achievements were limited. He did not play a leading role in the civil rights movement for fear of losing the support of southern Democrats (Dixiecrats, see page 26), who opposed civil rights, and he only stepped in with firm commitments after events in Birmingham (see page 39).

▲ **Source K** The leaders of the Washington March meeting President Kennedy, 28 August 1963. King is second on the left and Kennedy is fourth from the right

ACTIVITIES

1 Study Source I (page 44). Suggest reasons why the NAACP sent such a letter to President Kennedy.

2 Study Source K. Why was the black vote crucial to President Kennedy?

3 What did Robert Kennedy mean when he said 'If King loses, worse leaders are going to take his place.' Explain your answer.

4 Study Source J (page 44) and answer the following questions:
   a) What problems facing black Americans does President Kennedy highlight?
   b) What does he imply in the last sentence?

5 Investigate what happened when President Kennedy threatened legal action against the state of Louisiana for refusing to fund unsegregated schools. Did this threat work? What happened as a result?

6 Choose the three achievements of President Kennedy that you think are most important. Explain your choices.

? Practice question

How useful are Sources J and K for an enquiry into President Kennedy's involvement in the civil rights movement? Explain your answer, using Sources J and K and your knowledge of the historical context. (*For guidance, see pages 71–73.*)

6.5 President Johnson and the Civil Rights Act of 1964

Following the death of President Kennedy by assassination in November 1963, his successor, Lyndon B. Johnson, was able to push the Civil Rights Bill through the House of Representatives and the Senate, ensuring that those southern Democrats who opposed the bill would be counterbalanced by Republicans. Johnson had been in high-level politics since 1938 but he needed all his skills to persuade and cajole the Republicans to vote with him. He put forward his vision of a 'Great Society', which would attack racial injustice and poverty. This was in the same spirit as Kennedy's 'New Frontier'. There was deep shock within the USA at Kennedy's assassination, and there were some in Congress who voted sympathetically for the bill. Johnson also won some support in Congress because he was a southerner, from Texas.

President Johnson addressed both houses of Congress and said 'No memorial oration or eulogy could more eloquently honor President Kennedy's memory than the earliest possible passage of the Civil Rights Bill for which he fought so long.' Even though some of the Southern Democrat Senators employed the filibuster, Johnson was eventually able to win enough support after vice-president Humphrey won over wavering opponents.

The Civil Rights Act is seen as President Johnson's greatest achievement. However, there were many black Americans who criticised it as being insufficient and coming rather late in the day. Naturally, there were many white Americans in the South who resented it and sought to make it fail.

THE CIVIL RIGHTS ACT, 1964

- Segregation in hotels, motels, restaurants, lunch counters and theatres was banned.
- The Act placed the responsibility on the Federal Government to bring cases to court where discrimination still occurred.
- Any business engaged in transactions with the government would be monitored to ensure there was no discrimination.
- The Fair Employment Practices Committee, which had been set up during the Second World War, was established on a permanent basis.
- The Act created the Equal Employment Opportunity Commission (EEOC) to implement the law.

ACTIVITIES

1 Why do you think both black and white Americans were able to criticise the 1964 Civil Rights Act?

2 Study Source L. Write a newspaper article praising the passing of the Civil Rights Act. Write a headline for your article of about six words.

▼ **Source L** President Johnson signing the Civil Rights Act on 2 July 1964. Martin Luther King is standing behind him

6.6 Selma and the Voting Rights Act

The Civil Rights Act did not mean that black Americans could vote and they were still subject to voting restrictions not faced by white citizens (see page 8), so King and his colleagues decided to force the issue by embarking on another non-violent campaign. The town of Selma, Alabama, was to be the battleground, chosen because only 383 black Americans out of 15,000 had been able to register as voters.

There were two months of attempts to register black voters – and two months of rejections. King and his followers were subjected to beatings and arrests. One demonstrator was murdered. The sheriff of Selma, Jim Clark, had a reputation which matched that of Bull Connor in Birmingham (see page 38). King was hoping for a brutal reaction to his demonstrations because he knew that the press and television would again highlight the continued bigotry of the South.

The march from Selma

It was decided to hold a march from Selma to the state capital, Birmingham, in order to present to Governor Wallace a petition asking for voting rights. Governor Wallace banned the march but King was determined to take his supporters and lobby him.

The march began on 7 March but was stopped on the Edmund Pettus Bridge (see Source M) and the marchers were attacked by Sheriff Clark's men and state troopers. The marchers faced tear gas and clubs, and were forced to return to Selma. This became known as 'Bloody Sunday' and the event forced President Johnson's hand. Johnson decided to introduce a Bill to enfranchise black Americans. On 15 March, Johnson gave a speech to Congress asking for a Voting Rights Bill. Meanwhile, a second attempt to march to Montgomery began on 9 March but King turned the marchers back – he had agreed with President Johnson that he would avoid another violent confrontation with Clark.

Eventually it was agreed that a march from Selma to Montgomery would go ahead if it was peaceful. On 21 March, King led more than 25,000 people – the biggest march ever seen in the South.

ACTIVITIES ?

1 What can you learn from Source M about the civil rights march from Selma?

2 Was King justified in putting the lives of his followers at risk in the Selma marches? Explain your answer.

▼**Source M** The civil rights march to the Edmund Pettus Bridge, Selma, 1965

The Voting Rights Act, 1965

The success of the march created an atmosphere of optimism and in the summer of 1965, President Johnson introduced the Voting Rights Bill. This Act:

- ended literacy tests
- ensured federal agents could monitor registration – and step in if it was felt there was discrimination. It was presumed that if fewer than 50 per cent of all a state's voting-age citizens were registered then racial discrimination was being exercised.

By the end of 1965, 250,000 black Americans had registered (one-third were assisted by government monitors, who checked that the law was being followed). A further 750,000 registered by the end of 1968 (see Table 6.1 for further registered voters data). Furthermore, the number of elected black representatives increased rapidly after the bill was enacted.

King's policy of non-violence appeared to have worked. There was widespread support and sympathy from white Americans, and two key pieces of legislation had been introduced that removed discrimination and disenfranchisement.

Despite the success of King's methodology other groups were emerging that opposed King's idea of non-violence. There was a feeling among some that progress was slow and that, too often, King had been ready to make deals with the white authorities. These groups will be explored in Chapter 7.

▼ **Table 6.1 Registered voters in Southern states in the USA, 1969**

State	Percentage of white people registered	Percentage of black people registered
Alabama	94.6	61.3
Arkansas	81.6	77.9
Florida	94.2	67.0
Georgia	88.5	60.4
Louisiana	87.1	60.8
Mississippi	89.8	66.5
North Carolina	78.4	53.7
South Caroliina	71.5	54.6
Tennessee	92.0	92.1
Texas	61.8	73.1
Virginia	78.7	58.9
USA as a whole	80.4	64.8

ACTIVITIES ?

1 What can you learn from Table 6.1 about voters in the USA in 1969?

2 Re-read the sections on the Civil Rights Act (page 46) and the Voting Rights Act. Which do you think was the more important Act? Explain your answer.

Practice question

Explain why there was progress in the civil rights Movement in the years 1963–65.

You may use the following in your answer:
- The March on Washington
- President Kennedy

You **must** also use information of your own.

(For guidance, see pages 94–95.)

6.7 How far do you agree with one of the interpretations?

This section provides guidance on how to answer the question 'How far do you agree with one of the interpretations?'

Question

How far do you agree with Interpretation 1 about the causes of the riots in US cities in the 1960s?
Explain your answer, using both interpretations and your knowledge of the historical context.

> **Interpretation 1** From *Our Changing World: Modern World History From 1919*, Michael Scott-Baumann and David Platt, published in 1989
>
> Many African Americans refused to accept Martin Luther King's call for non-violence. They did not want to seek white support. ... The anger and frustration of urban African Americans erupted in riots. These often started with incidents involving the police. Tempers flared. Punches were thrown, rumours spread and knives were drawn. One such riot broke out in Watts, Los Angeles in 1965.

> **Interpretation 2** From *The Modern World 1914–80*, P. Sauvain, published in 1989
>
> Progress did not come fast enough for many militant African Americans, oppressed by the poverty of the slums and often unemployed. They resented the failure of many states to implement the Civil Rights laws and obey the rulings of the Supreme Court. 'We want Black Power' they said. Between 1965 and 1968 there were serious riots in the African American suburbs of over 100 US cities.

How to answer

You need to give a balanced answer which agrees and disagrees with the interpretation using evidence from the two interpretations as well as your own knowledge. An example is given below.

Step 1
State the view given in Interpretation 1 using evidence from the interpretation itself.

Example
Interpretation 1 supports the view that the riots began because people did not support King's approach and because of the attitude of the police.

Step 2
Agree with the view given in Interpretation 1 using your own knowledge. In answer to this question you would need to expand an the example answer with at least one more example of evidence from your own knowledge.

Example
Young African Americans were frustrated at the way whites were involved and SNCC leader, Carmichael, called for a challenge after having been arrested so many times. He wanted African Americans to resist the police. The Detroit and Newark riots were good examples of frustration and police insensitivity.

Step 3
Disagree with the view given in Interpretation 1 using evidence from Interpretation 2. In answer to this question you would need to expand on the example answer with at least one more example of evidence from Interpretation 2.

Example
Interpretation 2 challenges the view about issues with King's policy or the attitude of the police. It suggests that social and economic issues were the causes of the riots, together with certain states refusing to follow legal changes.

Step 4
Disagree with the view given in Interpretation 1 using your own knowledge. See if you can add to the example given with more evidence from your own knowledge.

Example
Groups such as the Black Panthers grew out of the opposition to King's methods - the Panthers were armed and preached violence. Even President Johnson recognised that continued oppression led to the riots.

Step 5
You now need to make a final judgement on the view given in Interpretation 1.

Example
Overall, I agree (or disagree) with the view given in Interpretation 2 because ...

6.8 Further examination practice on interpretations

Here is an opportunity to practise answering some more interpretation questions.

Source A Adapted from an interview with one of King's supporters in 1957

By the summer of 1956, some of Montgomery's business owners were frustrated with the boycott because it was costing them thousands of dollars. African Americans were not shopping as much in their stores. These shopkeepers wanted to keep segregation but their businesses were losing money. They even formed a group to negotiate with the boycotters but talks came to nothing. Economics had a lot to do with the end of the boycott.

Source B From an interview with James Farmer after the end of the Bus Boycott. Farmer was a civil rights activist and founder of CORE.

The Montgomery Bus Boycott had the charisma to capture the imagination of people. King had a combination of qualities: he was a Southern Baptist preacher, speaking with a Southern accent – that was important – who could preach. At the same time, he could address a Harvard audience and do it intelligently. How many preachers at that time – 1955, 1956 – knew of Gandhi and his work and could speak of non-violence? King was just perfect.

Interpretation 1 From *The American Tradition, A History of the United States*, R. Green, L. Becker and R. Covello, published in 1984

When Rosa Parks was arrested, the black community was outraged. The following day, black leaders met and planned the boycott. Martin Luther King, a young Baptist minister, was chosen to lead it. King was strongly influenced by the ideas of India's independence leader, Mohandas K. Gandhi. King asked the blacks of Montgomery to avoid violence and to practise civil disobedience. The black community supported King for a year by refusing to ride on the city buses. In December, the Supreme Court ruled that the Montgomery bus segregation law was unconstitutional. Because of the boycott, King became a nationally known figure.

Interpretation 2 From *World Powers in the Twentieth Century*, H. Ward, published in 1985

The most famous victory of the Civil Rights campaigns of these times (some of which were joined by white students from the North) was the 1955 Bus Boycott in Montgomery, organised by Martin Luther King. For a year, African Americans refused to ride on buses in which certain seats were reserved for whites only. The bus company nearly went broke because African Americans – the poorer end of the population – were the main customers. In the end the company gave in.

Question 1

Study Interpretations 1 and 2 about the reasons for the success of the Montgomery Bus Boycott. They give two views about the end of the Montgomery Bus Boycott. What is the main difference between the views? Explain your answer using details from both interpretations.

- You need to give the views of each interpretation and back these up with evidence from each one.

Question 2

Suggest **one** reason why Interpretations 1 and 2 give different views about the end of the Montgomery Bus Boycott. You may use Sources A and B to help explain your answer.

The interpretations may differ because:
- they have given weight to two different sources. You can use evidence from Sources A and B for this answer. Match the sources to the interpretations
- they are partial extracts and in this case they do not actually contradict one another
- the authors have a different emphasis.

Question 3

How far do you agree with Interpretation 2 about the end of the Montgomery Bus Boycott? Explain your answer, using both interpretations and your knowledge of the historical context.

You need to give a balanced answer which agrees and disagrees with the interpretation using evidence from the two interpretations as well as your own knowledge.
- Agree with the view with evidence from Interpretation 2.
- Agree with the view with evidence from your own knowledge.
- Disagree with the view with evidence from Interpretation 1.
- Disagree with the view with evidence from your own knowledge.
- Make a final judgement on the view.

7 Malcolm X and Black Power, 1963-70

The 1960s was a strange and paradoxical decade for the civil rights movement. There was support from presidents Kennedy and Johnson. Legislation such as the Civil Rights Act (see page 46) and the Voting Rights Act (see page 48) removed the major areas of discrimination. Moreover, Martin Luther King had raised the profile of the injustices that black Americans had to endure. On the other hand, the USA saw its worst racial violence and rioting during the years 1965–67. It also saw the rise of militant leaders such as Malcolm X, Bobby Seale and Huey Newton, and the formation of the paramilitary Black Panthers.

7.1 The role of Malcolm X in the civil rights movement

For some in the civil rights movement, progress had been painfully slow, and a feeling grew that King's methods would never bring equality either in politics or in opportunities in life. This frustration led to the development of a number of political groups, one of whom was made famous by Malcolm X.

The Black Muslims

A group that had never accepted King's ideas was the Black Muslims (also known as the **Nation of Islam**) – its supporters openly sought **separatism**. Members rejected their slave surnames and called themselves 'X'.

The most famous member of the Black Muslims was Malcolm X, and his brilliant oratorical skills helped increase membership of the group to about 100,000 in the years 1952–64. He was a superb organiser and during his membership of the Black Muslims, he travelled across the USA winning converts. Malcolm X helped set up educational and social programmes aimed at black youths in **ghettoes**. By 1960, more than 75 per cent of members of the Black Muslims were aged 17–35. Malcolm X is credited with reconnecting black Americans with their African heritage and is responsible for the spread of Islam in the black community in the USA. His influence on people such as Stokely Carmichael (see page 53) was crucial.

Malcolm X was never afraid to attack King and other leaders of the civil rights movement. He criticised the 1963 march on Washington (see Source A, page 52) and could not understand why so many black people were impressed by 'a demonstration run by whites in front of a statue of a president who has been dead for a hundred years and who didn't like us when he was alive'. Malcolm X had a tremendous influence on young urban black Americans. He felt that violence could be justified not only for self-defence but also as a means to secure a separate black nation.

MALCOLM X (BORN MALCOLM LITTLE), 1925–65

1925	Born Malcolm Little, in Omaha
1931	Father murdered by white supremacists
1942	Lived in New York, involved in pimping and drug dealing
1946	Found guilty of burglary and imprisoned
1952	Released from jail. Had become a follower of the Black Muslims. Changed his name to 'X'
1958	Married Betty Shabazz
1964	Left the Black Muslims and formed Muslim Mosque, Inc. and the Black Nationalist Organization of Afro-American Unity
1964	Went on pilgrimage to Mecca. His political and religious views altered. Changed his name to Malik El-Hajj Shabazz
1965	21 February, shot by three members of the Nation of Islam

Reactions to the Black Muslims

Many members of the mainstream civil rights groups did not like the Black Muslims, and some felt that the group had a 'hate-white doctrine', which was as dangerous as any white racist group. Thurgood Marshall (see page 9) said that the Black Muslims was run by a 'bunch of thugs organised from prisons and financed by some Arab group'. Such criticism did not concern Malcolm X.

> **Source A** Malcolm X, speaking in 1963 about the March on Washington
>
> Yes I was there. I observed that circus. Who ever heard of angry revolutionists all harmonising 'We shall overcome ... Sum Day ...' while tripping and swaying along arm-in-arm with the very people they were supposed to be angrily revolting against? Who ever heard of angry revolutionists swinging their bare feet together with their oppressor in lily-pad park pools, with gospels and guitars and 'I have a dream' speeches? And the black masses in America were – and still are – having a nightmare.

> **Source B** From a speech by Malcolm X in New York, 12 December 1964
>
> I believe in the brotherhood of man, all men, but I don't believe in brotherhood with anybody who doesn't want brotherhood with me. I believe in treating people right, but I'm not going to waste my time trying to treat somebody right who doesn't know how to return the treatment.

Malcolm X's later change of attitude

In 1964, after a visit to Mecca, Malcom X changed his views and left the Black Muslims to set up the Muslim Mosque Inc. and the Organization of Afro-American Unity to promote closer ties between Africans and African-Americans. He said the trip to Mecca allowed him to see Muslims of different races interacting as equals. He came to believe that Islam could be the means by which racial problems could be overcome. He pushed to end racial **discrimination** in the USA, but this brought him enemies, particularly among the Black Muslims. Malcolm X's views and ideas became the foundation of the more radical movements such as Black Power (see page 53) and the Black Panthers (see page 55). Many historians have said that Malcolm X helped raise the self-esteem of black Americans more than any other individual in the civil rights movement.

Assassination

Malcolm X was assassinated by three Black Muslims on 21 February 1965. He was shot several times as he began a speech to 400 of his followers at the Audubon Ballroom just outside the district of Harlem in New York. During the week before his assassination, Malcolm X and his family survived the firebombing of their home in the Queen's district of New York. In March 1966, two members of the Black Muslims were found guilty of Malcolm X's murder.

> **Source C** From Malcolm X's speech at the founding rally of the Organization of Afro-American Unity, 28 June 1964
>
> We have formed an organization known as the Organization of Afro-American Unity, which has the same aim and objective to fight whoever gets in our way, to bring about the complete independence of people of African descent here in the Western Hemisphere, and first here in the United States, and bring about the freedom of these people by any means necessary. That's our motto. We want freedom by any means necessary. We want justice by any means necessary. We want equality by any means necessary.

> **Source D** From Malcolm X's funeral oration, given by the black American actor Ossie Davis
>
> Many will ask what Harlem finds to honor in this stormy, controversial and bold young captain – and we will smile. They will say he is of hate – a fanatic, a racist ... and we will answer 'Did you ever talk to Brother Malcolm? Did you ever really listen to him? Did he ever do a mean thing? Was he ever associated with violence or any public disturbance?' ... in honoring him, we honor the best in ourselves.

ACTIVITIES

1 Study Source A. What was Malcolm X's attitude towards the march on Washington?

2 Study Source B. What does this source tell you about Malcolm X's beliefs?

3 Why was it important for the Nation of Islam to offer educational and social programmes?

4 To whom was Malcolm X referring when he said '... a president who has been dead for a hundred years'?

5 Study Source C. Why were many Americans concerned by the phrase 'by any means necessary'?

6 How reliable is Source D about Malcolm X? Explain your answer using the sources and your own knowledge.

Practice questions

1 Give two things you can infer from Source D about Malcolm X. (For guidance, see page 79.)

2 How useful are Sources A and C for an enquiry into Malcolm X's attitude to securing improved civil rights? Explain your answer, using Sources A and C and your knowledge of the historical context. *(For guidance, see pages 71–73.)*

7.2 Stokely Carmichael and the emergence of Black Power

During the years 1965–67, there were riots in many cities across the USA. Perhaps the worst was in the Watts district of Los Angeles. The riots saw the deaths of more than 30 people, hundreds of arrests and millions of dollars' worth of damage (see page 57). The Black Power movement emerged against this backdrop of urban unrest. It was originally a political slogan but in the late 1960s it came to cover a wide range of activities that aimed to increase the power of blacks in American life. Stokely Carmichael (see box) and others in the **Student Non-Violent Coordinating Committee (SNCC)** wanted blacks to take responsibility for their own lives and rejected white help. For some black activists, Black Power meant separatism, but for others it was a way of ridding the USA of a corrupt power structure. Carmichael and his associates wanted black Americans to create their own political force so that they would not have to rely on the black groupings that existed at the time, such as the **NAACP, CORE** and the **SCLC**.

Carmichael and his followers wanted blacks to have pride in their heritage. They promoted African forms of dress and appearance, and adopted the slogan 'Black is beautiful'.

Carmichael attracted criticism because of his aggressive attitude, and was attacked when he denounced the involvement of the USA in the Vietnam War. He eventually left the SNCC and became associated with the Black Panthers (see page 55), but left the USA and moved to Guinea in 1969, where he lived until his death in 1998.

▲ Stokely Carmichael, leader of the SNCC and who later joined the Black Panthers

STOKELY CARMICHAEL, 1941–98

1941	Born in Port of Spain, Trinidad and Tobago
1943	Moved to New York City
1960	Attended Howard University, Washington, DC. Gained a degree in Philosophy.
1961	Took part in the Freedom Rides, jailed for seven weeks
1966	Chairman of the SNCC
1966	Twenty-seventh arrest – made his 'Black Power' speech
1967	Wrote *Black Power*
1968	Joined Black Panthers
1969	Left the USA, moved to Guinea. Changed his name to Kwame Ture.
1998	Died in Guinea

Source E From a speech made in 1966 by Stokely Carmichael, leader of the Student Non-violent Coordinating Committee, describing his own frustrations and those of many black Americans. He had just been released from police custody following involvement in a civil rights march in Mississippi

This is the twenty-seventh time I have been arrested. I ain't going to jail no more. The only way we gonna stop them white men from whuppin' us is to take over. We been saying freedom for six years and we aint got nothin'. What we gonna start sayin' now is Black Power!

ACTIVITIES ?

1 What is meant by the term 'Black Power'?
2 Write a speech for an SNCC meeting. In it explain why you have now rejected King's approach and agree with the ideas of Stokely Carmichael.

Practice question

Give two things you can infer from Source E about Stokely Carmichael. (*For guidance, see page 79.*)

7.3 The 1968 Mexico Olympics

The Black Power movement gained tremendous publicity at the 1968 Mexico Olympics, at the winners' ceremony for the men's 200 m and 400 m relay. The athletes wore part of the movement's uniform – a single black glove and a black beret – and also gave the clenched-fist salute. During the ceremony, when the US national anthem was being played, Tommie Smith gave the salute with his right hand to indicate Black Power and John Carlos with his left to show black unity. Smith also wore a black scarf to represent black pride, and black socks with no shoes to represent black poverty in racist America. Their action created such a furore that, following the ceremony, Smith and Carlos were banned from the athlete's village and sent back to the USA. They were accused of bringing politics into sport and damaging the Olympic spirit. On their return, they both received several death threats. As a result of this sporting event, the whole world became aware of the Black Power movement.

▲ **Source F** Tommie Smith and John Carlos at the 1968 Olympic Games. Smith won the gold and Carlos the bronze in the 200 metres

▲ **Source G** The US 400 metres relay team at the 1968 Olympic Games, giving the Black Power salute and wearing the movement's black berets

> **Source H** From a press conference given by Tommie Smith in October 1968, following the Olympic medal ceremony
>
> If I win, I am American, not a black American. But if I did something bad, then they would say I am a Negro. We are black and we are proud of being black. Black America will understand what we did tonight.

> **Source I** From an article in *Time* magazine criticising the actions of Smith and Carlos. The title of the article was *Angrier, Nastier, Uglier.* (The official Olympic motto was Faster, Higher, Stronger')
>
> ... Smith and Carlos are two disaffected black athletes from the US who put on a public display of petulance that sparked one of the most unpleasant controversies in Olympic history and turned the high drama of the games into theatre of the absurd.

Practice question

1 Give two things you can learn from Source F about Black Power. (*For guidance, see page 79.*)
2 How useful are Sources H and I for an enquiry into the reasons for the Black Power demonstration at the Olympic Games? Explain your answer, using Sources H and I and your own knowledge of the historical context. (*For guidance, see pages 71–73.*)

ACTIVITY

Working in groups, prepare a case to support or condemn the US athletes at the Mexico Olympics in 1968.

7.4 The Black Panther movement

At the same time as the urban riots and the development of 'Black Power', there emerged the **Black Panther Party**. This was founded by Huey Newton and Bobby Seale in October 1966 in Oakland, California (see Source J). Both of these men had been heavily influenced by Malcolm X.

Eldridge Cleaver, the party's Minister of Information, wrote *Soul on Ice* (1967), which included the ten-point programme of the Panthers aims (see Source K). The Black Panthers were prepared to use revolutionary means to achieve these aims. They were even prepared to form alliances with radical white groups if they felt it would help bring down the 'establishment'. The leaders of the Panthers advocated an end to **capitalism** and the establishment of a socialist society. Seale constantly stated: 'We believe our fight is a class struggle and not a race struggle.'

The Panthers wore uniforms and were ready to use weapons, training members in their use. By the end of 1968, they had 5,000 members. However, internal divisions and the events of 1969 – which saw 27 Panthers killed and 700 injured in confrontations with the police – resulted in diminishing support. The group was constantly targeted by the FBI and by 1982 the Black Panthers had disbanded.

▲ **Source J** Bobby Seale (left) and Huey Newton, co-founders of the Black Panther Party for Self-Defence

Source K The Black Panthers' ten-point programme, October 1966

We want:

1 Freedom. We want power to determine the destiny of our Black Community.
2 We want full employment for our people.
3 We want an end to the robbery by the white man of our Black Community.
4 We want decent housing, fit for shelter of human beings.
5 We want education for our people that exposes the true nature of this decadent American society. We want education that teaches us our true history and our role in the present-day society.
6 We want all black men to be exempt from military service.
7 We want an immediate end to police brutality and murder of black people.
8 We want freedom for all black men held in federal, state, county and city prisons and jails.
9 We want all black people when brought to trial to be tried in court by a jury of their peer group or people from their black communities, as defined by the Constitution of the United States.
10 We want land, bread, housing, education, clothing, justice and peace.

ACTIVITIES ?

1 What can you learn from Source J about the Black Panthers?

2 Study Source K. Which of these aims do you think that Martin Luther King would have opposed?

Source L From *Revolutionary Suicide* (1973) by Huey Newton

We had seen Watts rise up the previous year. We had seen how the police attacked the Watts community after causing the trouble in the first place. We had seen Martin Luther King come to Watts in an effort to calm the people, and we had seen his philosophy of non-violence rejected. Black people had been taught non-violence; it was deep in us.

What good, however, was non-violence when the police were determined to rule by force? We had seen all this, and we recognized that the rising consciousness of Black people was almost at the point of explosion. Out of this need sprang the Black Panther Party. Bobby Seale and I finally had no choice but to form an organization that would involve the lower-class brothers.

The achievements of the Black Panthers

Despite constant harassment from the FBI and police (see Source N), the Black Panthers were able to point to some successes during their existence. They established the 'Free Breakfast for Children Program' in parts of California and Chicago. In addition, they provided clothing distribution centres, gave guidance on drugs re-habilitation and assistance to those who had relatives in prison.

▲ **Source M** Symbol of the Black Panther Party

Source N J. Edgar Hoover, FBI Director, quoted in the *New York Times*, 9 September 1968

The Black Panthers are the greatest threat to the internal security of the country. Schooled in communist ideology and the teaching of Chinese Communist leader Mao Tse-tung, its members have perpetrated numerous assaults on police officers and have engaged in violent confrontations with police throughout the country. Leaders and representatives of the Black Panther Party travel extensively all over the United States preaching their gospel of hate and violence not only to ghetto residents, but to students in colleges, universities and high schools as well.

Practice question

1 How useful are Sources L (page 55) and N for an enquiry into the Black Panther Movement? Explain your answer, using Sources L and N and your knowledge of the historical context. *(For guidance, see pages 71–73.)*

2 Explain why the civil rights movements changed to more extreme methods in the years 1963–70.

You may use the following in your answer:
- Malcolm X
- The Black Panthers

You **must** also use information of your own.

(For guidance, see pages 94–95.)

ACTIVITIES

1 What image does Source M project of the Black Panthers?

2 Work in pairs and read pages 55–56. Present a case to show that the Black Power movement and the Black Panthers were a threat to the security of US society in the 1960s.

3 Make a copy of and complete the following table.

	Similarities	Differences
Malcolm X	He was prepared to use violence when necessary.	
Stokely Carmichael/Black Power		
Black Panthers		

There were further significant developments in the civil rights movement in the years 1965 to 1975. Serious inner city riots in the Watts District of Los Angeles precipitated the Kerner Report of 1967, which highlighted the economic issues faced by black Americans. Martin Luther King became far more active in trying to improve the economic and social position of black Americans in the North, more especially in Chicago, but with limited success. His assassination in 1968 led to a further outbreak of violence. Despite this, black Americans continued to make some, if limited, political, economic and social progress in the later 1960s and early 1970s.

8.1 The riots of 1965–67 and the Kerner Report, 1968

Despite the Civil Rights Acts passed in 1957 and 1964 (see pages 21 and 46), many young black Americans were frustrated, and those who lived in the ghettoes felt anger at the high rates of unemployment, continuing discrimination and poverty they experienced. During the three summers of riots between 1965 and 1967, more than 130 people were killed and the damage totalled more than $700 million.

The Watts riot

On 11 August 1965, the frustration exploded into a major riot in the Watts district of Los Angeles. The riot involved 30,000 people, left 34 dead, 1,072 injured, 4,000 arrested and caused about $40 million of damage.

After the Watts riot, President Johnson is alleged to have said to one of his press secretaries: 'What did you expect? I don't know why we're so surprised. When you put your foot on a man's neck and hold him down for three hundred years, and then you let him up, what's he going to do? He's going to knock your block off.'

Martin Luther King visited Watts and was shocked and surprised by what he saw. Many of the black Americans he met were triumphant and claimed they had been successful in the riot. King felt that much of his work had been undone and he said: 'We obviously are not reaching these people.'

▲ **Source A** Police officers during the Watts riot, 1965

> **Source B President Johnson speaking to Congress about the Watts riots**
>
> Who of you could have predicted 10 years ago, that in this last, sweltering, August week thousands upon thousands of disenfranchised black American men and women would suddenly take part in self-government, and that thousands more in that same week would strike out in an unparalleled act of violence … It is our duty – and it is our desire – to open our hearts to humanity's cry for help. It is our obligation to seek to understand what could lie beneath the flames that scarred that great city. So let us equip the poor and the oppressed – let us equip them for the long march to dignity and to wellbeing. But let us never confuse the need for decent work and fair treatment with an excuse to destroy and to uproot.

Further riots

There were further riots across the USA's major cities in the summers of 1966 and 1967. Many followed a similar pattern – the arrest of a black youth, a police raid, rumours of police brutality and then the explosion of the riot. Racial violence peaked in the summer of 1967, when there were race riots in 125 US cities. The two largest riots occurred less than two weeks apart in July: riots in Newark (see Source C) left 26 dead and over 1,000 injured, while the Detroit riots resulted in more than 40 dead, hundreds injured and 7,000 arrested.

▲ **Source C** Looters being arrested after the riots in Newark, 1967

ACTIVITIES

1 What can you learn from Source A about the riot in Watts?

2 Study Source B. What can you learn from this source about President Johnson?

3 Which do you think were the two most important causes of the riots? Explain your answer.

4 Study Source C. Can you suggest reasons why leaders of the civil rights movement condemned the looting?

5 What was the significance of the Kerner Report (Source D)?

Practice question

1 How useful are Sources A and B for an enquiry into the Watts riot? Explain your answer, using Sources A and B and your knowledge of the historical context. (*For guidance, see pages 71–73.*)

2 Give two things you can infer from Source D about the Kerner Report. (*For guidance, see page 79.*)

The Kerner Report

The riots of 1965–67 caused President Johnson and his advisers to investigate the factors behind them. The National Advisory Commission on Civil Disorders was set up and published the Kerner Report in 1968 (named after Otto Kerner, the Chair of the Commission). The Black Power movement had made it clear that equality of opportunity did not exist and the Kerner Report (1968) stated that racism was deeply embedded in American society. It also concluded that the USA was, 'moving toward two societies, one black, one white – separate and unequal.'

This report not only highlighted the economic issues faced by black Americans, but also the systematic police bias and brutality. The Kerner Report recommended sweeping federal initiatives that would mean increased expenditure. Following the election of President Richard Nixon later that year, the report was largely ignored.

> **Source D** Extracts from the Kerner Report, 1968
>
> Certain fundamental matters are clear. Of these, the most fundamental is the racial attitude and behaviour of white Americans toward black Americans. Race prejudice has shaped our history decisively; it now threatens to affect our future.
>
> White racism is essentially responsible for the explosive mixture which has been accumulating in our cities since the end of World War II. Among the ingredients of this mixture are:
>
> - Pervasive discrimination and segregation in employment, education and housing, which have resulted in the continuing exclusion of great numbers of Back Americans from the benefits of economic progress …
> - Black in-migration and white exodus, which have produced the massive and growing concentrations of impoverished black Americans in our major cities, creating a growing crisis of deteriorating facilities and services and unmet human needs …
>
> The frustrations of powerlessness have led some black Americans to the conviction that there is no effective alternative to violence as a means of achieving redress of grievances, and of 'moving the system'.
>
> The police are not merely a spark factor. To some black Americans police have come to symbolize white power, white racism and white repression. And the fact is that many police do reflect and express these white attitudes. The atmosphere of hostility and cynicism is reinforced by a widespread belief among black Americans in the existence of police brutality and in a 'double standard' of justice and protection – one for black Americans and one for whites.
>
> … we have seen in our cities a chain reaction of racial violence. If we are heedless, none of us shall escape the consequences.

8.2 King's campaign in the North

King and some of the SCLC (see page 20) felt that they had not won over black Americans in the North. King visited the Los Angeles' Watts ghetto after the black riot of 1965 (see page 53) and began to change his views about what was meant by 'freedom'. He had seen this as essentially securing the vote for black Americans and removing segregation and discrimination, especially in the South. He now increasingly focused on the need for economic freedom for black Americans, especially in the Northern states. King wanted to achieve a fairer distribution of wealth to reduce the massive differences in wealth in America and get rid of poverty (see Source E).

> **Source E From a speech by Martin Luther King**
> It is much easier to integrate lunch counters than it is to eradicate slums. It's much easier to guarantee the right to vote than it is to guarantee an annual minimum income and create jobs.

The Chicago Freedom Movement

In January 1966, King and his supporters decided to create the Chicago Freedom Movement, with the aim of removing segregation within that city. King was keen to show that non-violence and non-violent direct action could bring change in society outside the South. This meant moving the focus of his work from the South to the North where black Americans had serious concerns about economic and social issues. Chicago was chosen because it had a population of 4 million people and almost one quarter of them were black, with most living in ghettoes in confined areas of the city. There was poor housing and education as well as high unemployment.

Opposition to King

King decided to use the same methods he had used in the past, more especially marches and publicity, believing these would bring about improvements. He did gain publicity but his methods were not successful. King worked in Chicago for most of 1966 and he and his followers were surprised by the open hostility of many whites in Chicago. There was a particularly serious attack on King during one march in Chicago where he was struck by a brick, although not badly injured. His desire for a fairer and more equal distribution of wealth was seen as too extreme, almost communist, by most Americans, who believed strongly in the capitalist system. Although many Northern whites and the Northern white churches often supported change in the South, they were less keen on economic and social changes that could mean they would have to pay higher taxes. Many whites, especially in Chicago, feared a fall in house prices if blacks moved into their neighbourhood.

When 500 blacks marched into a white Chicago neighbourhood to highlight the fact that they were unable to live there, the white residents threw rocks and bottles at them. The police gave the black marchers little or no protection. Some argued that King had worsened the situation in Chicago, encouraging a white backlash against black Americans who were increasingly seen as troublemakers. King also faced opposition from Chicago's Mayor Daley who resented his interference in his city and the *Chicago Tribune* which described King as a 'paid professional agitator'.

Achievements in the North

Some successes were made in the North, especially in housing and the provision of mortgages for black Americans, although they were short-lived. Daley agreed to encourage integrated housing in Chicago but little was achieved with most blacks remaining in the ghetto. The SCLC did receive a $4 million federal grant to improve Chicago housing but again there were few lasting achievements. In autumn 1966, King left Chicago. Jesse Jackson, a leading member of the SCLC, took over the leadership of what became known as 'Operation Breadbasket', which successfully used economic boycotts to increase black employment.

King's interest in the North seemed to lessen and in 1967, he became more involved with the anti-Vietnam War Movement and also the issue of poverty in the USA.

> **Source F From an interview with Linda Brant Hall in 1998. She lived in Chicago and was a member of CORE**
> When King came he wanted to work with just one umbrella group. And then he did not understand that each group within that group had a program of its own – had leaders of its own, had its own kind of direction that it was going in; but we all had a common goal and needed somebody like King. We needed him to lend us his strength, to lend us his name. So, when he came in to try and discount what was already here, I think, he offended quite a few people.

ACTIVITY

1 Using a mind map summarise King's campaign in the North, including his aims, successes and failures.

2 Why was there so much opposition in Chicago to his campaign?

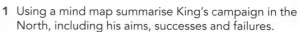

Practice question

How useful are Sources E and F as evidence of King's campaign in the North? Explain your answer, using Sources E and F and your knowledge of the historical context. (*For guidance, see pages 71–73.*)

8.3 The assassination of Martin Luther King

On 4 April 1968, Martin Luther King was visiting Memphis in support of black refuse collectors, who were striking for equal treatment with their white co-workers. This was an indication that social and economic issues were becoming increasingly important to the civil rights movement.

The economic and educational gulf between blacks and whites was still great, not only in the South but also in the North. However, King was finding it increasingly difficult to control his followers, who struggled with his principle of non-violence. King was assassinated that day in Memphis. James Earl Ray, a white racist, was arrested and jailed for the crime, but there is still doubt over whether he was the real killer.

On 3 April 1968 (the day before his assassination), King gave a speech at a church rally in which he spoke of his hopes and fears for the future. At the end of the long speech he spoke of 'having been to the mountain top' and said '… we as people will get to the Promised Land!' Prophetically, King said he was not concerned about living a long life.

King's funeral was held on 9 April 1968 at the Ebenezer Baptist Church in Atlanta (see Source G). About 100,000 people came for the service, though the church could only hold 800. After the funeral, a mule-drawn wagon carried King's body through Atlanta's streets to Morehouse College, followed by up to 200,000 mourners.

The impact of the assassination

Following Martin Luther King's death, there was a final outburst of rioting across the country. Forty-six people died, more than 3,000 were injured in violent clashes and there were demonstrations in more than 100 cities. More than 21,000 people were arrested and it was estimated that almost $70 million worth of property was damaged. This violence was a great irony – it seemed as if King's whole work and life had been for nothing.

The year 1968 seemed to mark the end of an era. Richard Nixon had won the presidential election, the Vietnam War had begun to dominate the domestic scene and the student movement also took centre stage.

There had been significant changes in the rights and equalities of black Americans, with legislation introduced in the 1960s giving equality and protection before the law. Despite this, the riots of 1965–67 and those that occurred on the death of King in 1968 indicated that there was still huge frustration among the black population.

In 1983, President Reagan established Martin Luther King Day as a national holiday, to be held on the third Monday in January.

ACTIVITIES

1 Find King's 'I have been to the mountain top' speech on the Martin Luther King Center website. What do you think he meant when he said 'We as a people will get to the Promised Land!'?

2 Can you suggest why there were riots across the USA on the death of Martin Luther King?

3 Write a speech for President Reagan outlining why Martin Luther King was to be remembered in the USA by means of a national holiday.

◀ **Source G** The funeral of Martin Luther King. This was the first of two funeral services held on 9 April 1968 in Atlanta. The first was at Ebenezer Baptist Church and the second was at Morehouse College

8.4 The extent of progress in civil rights by 1975

During the period 1968–75 there was some progress in the civil rights movement, but it was limited. Above all else, by 1975, the civil rights movement had succeeded in encouraging much greater federal intervention on behalf of black Americans.

Nixon and civil rights

Richard Nixon had seemed to be in favour of civil rights in the 1950s. As president (1969–74), however, he showed little sympathy or support for the movement. He made no attempt to meet black leaders and was against the idea that there should be a national holiday to celebrate King's birthday. He dealt harshly with extreme groups such as the Black Panthers (see page 55).

Progress in education

Despite these obstacles, there was some progress in integration during this period. In 1968, 68 per cent of Southern black children attended segregated schools, but by 1974, this had fallen to 8 per cent. The bussing initiative made Southern schools among America's best integrated. Nixon refused to support the Supreme Court during the *Swann v Charlotte-Mecklenburg case* of 1971. The Court said it was time for school **desegregation** to be fully carried out by bussing children considerable distances to achieve racially mixed schools. However, Nixon insisted that this would not benefit the children involved, nor the local community.

Progress in employment and business

In 1972, Nixon set up the Office of Minority Business Enterprise to encourage black businesses. In the same year, the Equal Employment Opportunity Act gave the courts greater powers to enforce equality in employment. Over 300,000 companies which had federal contracts now employed more black Americans.

By 1975, African Americans could point to some progress but also to continued inequalities. In 1970, unemployment among whites was, on average, about 5 per cent but for black Americans it was almost 8 per cent (see Figure 8.1). Among white teenagers, it was about 15 per cent but for black American teenagers it was about 50 per cent.

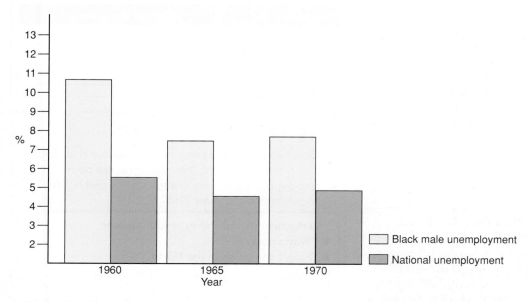

▲ **Figure 8.1** Black American and national unemployment figures in the years 1960–70

Progress in politics

In 1973, more than 200 African Americans were elected to state legislatures and 16 had been elected to Congress. However, in the 1976 presidential election more than one third of African Americans did not register to vote and fewer than half of those registered actually voted. Among the under 25s, just over one third registered to vote and only one quarter of those voted. It was pleasing to note gains in the South, where elections showed not only increased black voter participation, but also increased involvement in politics (see Figure 8.2). Nationally, the picture looked very healthy, however the figures shown in Figure 8.2 do disguise the failure to secure increased numbers in Congress.

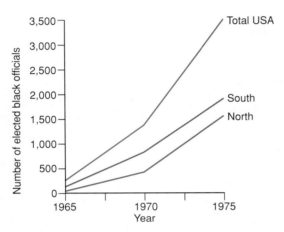

▲ **Figure 8.2** Graph showing elected black officials, 1965–75

Poverty

Statistics suggest that federal anti-poverty measures raised the living standards of black Americans. In 1960, 50 per cent of black Americans were living below the poverty line. This had fallen to 30 per cent by 1974. Source H and Table 8.1 indicate that progress was made in terms of employment opportunities for African Americans. Moreover, Table 8.2 shows that aspirations had also changed for them. Educational opportunities had also improved, offering a way out of the poverty trap.

Source H From an article about civil rights in a British history magazine for GCSE students

There were definite improvements in the quality of life for many of America's disadvantaged; in 1965, 19 per cent of black Americans earned the average wage, by 1967, this had risen to 27 per cent; in 1960, the average educated age of a black American was 10.8, by 1967 this had increased to 12.2.

▼ **Table 8.1** The percentage of people living in poverty in the USA in the years 1959–68

	1959	1963	1966	1968
Whole population	22.4	19.5	14.7	12.8
Whites	18.1	15.3	11.3	10.0
Non-whites	56.2	51.0	39.8	33.5

▼ **Table 8.2** The distribution of white and black American family annual income, 1976 (figures are given in percentages)

Income in $	White families %	African American families %
Under 3,000	3.1	10.1
3,000–4,999	5.3	16.0
5,000–5,999	7.3	12.5
7,000–8,999	7.8	10.3
9,000–11,999	11.9	12.2
12,000–14,999	12.3	11.3
15,000–19,999	19.8	13.4
20,000 and over	32.5	14.2

ACTIVITIES

1 What does Figure 8.2 suggest about black Americans and politics?

2 Study Source H, Figures 8.1 and 8.2 and Tables 8.1 and 8.2. Working in pairs, make a copy of and complete the following table about the progress made by African Americans in the years 1960–75. One of you should complete the section on progress and the other on lack of progress.

Progress	Lack of progress

Practice question

1 Give two things you can infer from Source H about the civil rights movement. (*For guidance, see page 79.*)

2 Explain why there were changes in the civil rights movement in the years 1965–75.

You may use the following in your answer:
- Watts riots
- King's campaign in the North

You **must** also use information of your own.

(*For guidance, see pages 94–95.*)

US involvement in the Vietnam War, 1954–75

This key topic examines the key developments in US involvement in Vietnam in the years 1954–75. The USA first became involved in Vietnam after the French defeat at Dien Bien Phu in 1954, but this involvement intensified in the 1960s under successive American presidents. Kennedy tried, unsuccessfully, to limit this involvement with his Strategic Hamlets Policy but it escalated greatly under Johnson in the years 1964–68. Increasing opposition to the war led to further change under Nixon, who tried to reduce US commitment with a policy of Vietnamisation.

Each chapter within this key topic explains a key issue and examines important lines of enquiry as outlined below.

There will also be guidance on how to answer the utility question (pages 71–73) and the inference question (page 79).

CHAPTER 9 REASONS FOR US INVOLVEMENT IN THE CONFLICT IN VIETNAM, 1954–63

- The battle of Dien Bien Phu and the end of French rule in Vietnam.
- Reasons for greater US involvement under Eisenhower, including the domino theory and the weaknesses of the Diem government.
- Greater involvement under Kennedy, including the overthrow of Diem and the Strategic Hamlet policy.
- Escalation under Johnson and the Gulf of Tonkin incident.

CHAPTER 10 THE NATURE OF THE CONFLICT IN VIETNAM, 1964–68

- The increasing threat of the Vietcong and increased US involvement in Vietnam.
- The guerrilla tactics used by the Vietcong.
- The methods used by the USA, including Search and Destroy, Operation Rolling Thunder and chemical weapons.
- The key features and significance of the Tet Offensive, 1968.

CHAPTER 11 CHANGES UNDER NIXON, 1969–73

- The key features of Vietnamisation. Reasons for its failure.
- The Nixon Doctrine and the withdrawal of US troops.
- Attacks on Cambodia, 1970, and Laos, 1971, and the bombing of North Vietnam, 1972.

TIMELINE 1954–75

1954	The defeat of the French at Dien Bien Phu	1964	The Gulf of Tonkin incident
1955	Diem elected president of South Vietnam	1965	Beginning of 'Operation Rolling Thunder'
1960	Ho Chi Minh set up the Vietcong to oppose Diem	1968	The Tet Offensive and the My Lai massacre
1962	The introduction of the Strategic Hamlet policy	1969	Introduction of Vietnamisation
		1970	Attacks on Cambodia
1963	Diem overthrown	1971	Attacks on Laos
		1972	The bombing of North Vietnam

Before the Second World War (1939–45), Vietnam was a French colony. In the years following the Second World War, the people of Vietnam overthrew the rule of France but divided the country into North Vietnam, under communist control, and South Vietnam, supported by the West. The country became another testing ground for communism and capitalism in the Cold War and the US became increasingly involved in the 1950s and early 1960s.

9.1 Origins of the conflict

The conflict in Vietnam had its origins in developments during and after the Second World War.

In 1939 Vietnam was part of an area known as French Indo-China (see Figure 9.1). This included contemporary Vietnam, Laos and Cambodia. French rule was harsh and unpopular, leading to uprisings such as that of 1930, led by the Nationalist Party of Vietnam. Such attempts were brutally crushed by the French.

Japan invaded and occupied Indo-China in 1940. Some in Vietnam saw this as the ideal opportunity to overthrow French rule and achieve independence. In 1941, two leading Vietnamese **communists**, Ho Chi Minh and Nguyen Vo Giap, a history teacher, set up the League for the Independence of Vietnam (or **Vietminh**) in southern China. Their aim was to establish an independent Vietnam, free from French and Japanese rule.

The US Intelligence Service helped by training and equipping the Vietminh and, by 1944, it was ready to begin **guerrilla** operations against the Japanese in North Vietnam. These were essentially small-scale attacks that were very successful and increased support for the Vietminh which, by 1945, had 5,000 guerrilla fighters. In August 1945 the Japanese were defeated in the Second World War and forced to evacuate all their conquests, including Vietnam.

▲ **Figure 9.1** Map showing French Indo-China in 1939. French Indo-China comprised modern-day Vietnam, Laos and Cambodia

HO CHI MINH, 1890–1969

Ho Chi Minh was born in central Vietnam in 1890 and went to school in Hué. He worked as a cook aboard a French steamship and, in the years before the outbreak of the First World War, lived in London and Paris where he helped to set up the French Communist Party. He went to China in 1924 where he established the Indo-Chinese Communist Party and worked to bring about an independent, communist Vietnam. In 1941 he was the joint founder of the Vietminh movement, fighting for independence. He continued to fight against the French in the years after the Second World War and played a major part in the defeat of France at Dien Bien Phu in 1954 (see page 65). He thus became President of North Vietnam. For the next fifteen years, until his death in 1969, he led the North Vietnamese battle to reunite North and South Vietnam. In 1975, Saigon, the former capital of South Vietnam, was renamed Ho Chi Minh City in his honour.

The post-war settlement

In September 1945, Ho Chi Minh quickly occupied the two leading cities of Hanoi and Saigon, and announced that Vietnam was an independent and democratic republic. At first, the USA, who did not want to see the restoration of the old colonial empires, sympathised with Ho Chi Minh and the idea of an independent Vietnam.

The new independent republic was, however, short-lived, as within weeks the French had moved 50,000 troops into Indo-China. The French quickly restored control over South Vietnam, where the Vietminh were not strong, and drove Ho Chi Minh and his followers into the jungles of North Vietnam. For the next five years Ho Chi Minh conducted another guerrilla campaign, this time against the French.

Developments in China

In 1949 the Chinese Communist Party, led by Mao Zedong, successfully won their civil war and established a communist government. This brought two major developments for events in Vietnam:

- Mao supported the Vietminh with essential military supplies such as artillery.
- A change in US policy (see page 66) – the USA now feared that communism would sweep across Asia and switched their support to the French. In 1950 President Truman agreed to send the French $15 million of supplies. Over the next four years the USA spent nearly $3 billion in helping the French.

The battle of Dien Bien Phu

The Vietminh led by Ho Chi Minh and Giap continued their guerrilla campaign against the French, although from 1951 they moved on from guerrilla-style fighting to big attacks on well-defended French positions.

The decisive battle for control of Vietnam took place at the French garrison of Dien Bien Phu. The French army established a fortified camp by air-lifting soldiers adjacent to a key Vietminh supply line to Laos. The plan was to cut off Vietminh soldiers fighting in Laos and force them to withdraw. The Vietminh, however, surrounded the camp and set up gun positions on the nearby hills, preventing the French from bringing in supplies. After two months, in May 1954, the French surrendered. After another two months, an armistice was signed and the French agreed to leave Indo-China. There had been 16,500 French troops at Dien Bien Phu. Only 3,000 lived to tell the story.

ACTIVITIES

1 Create a mind map showing why the French were forced to leave Vietnam.

2 The following account of events in Vietnam before 1954 has been written by someone who is not clear about key developments. Re-write the account and replace any errors in fact.

> Vietnam was part of the area known as Indo-China, which also included Laos and Indonesia. This was controlled by the Japanese in the years before 1939. In 1943 the French invaded and took over Indo-China. The Indo-Chinese Communist Party led by Mao Zedong fought against these invaders. When the French were defeated in 1945, Mao Zedong took over South Vietnam.

3 Put together a flow chart to show the main developments in Vietnam in the years 1940–54.

◄ Source A The Vietminh taking the spoils of victory after Dien Bien Phu

9.2 Greater US involvement under Eisenhower

During the 1950s the USA became far more involved in Vietnam as part of their policy of **containment** to stop the spread of communism. In the years after 1947, President Truman was determined to 'get tough' on the Soviet Union and stop the spread of communism. This became known as containment and was stated clearly in the **Truman Doctrine** of 1947, which promised to support all 'peoples who resist being enslaved by armed minorities or outside pressure or communism'.

The Geneva Agreement

In May 1954, after the battle of Dien Bien Phu, Britain, France, China, the Soviet Union, the USA and Vietnam met in Geneva, Switzerland, to decide the future of Vietnam. The following points were agreed:

■ Vietnam would be divided temporarily along the 17th parallel into North and South Vietnam (see Figure 9.2, page 69).
■ North Vietnam would be led by Ho Chi Minh and the South would be led by Ngo Dinh Diem.
■ Vietminh forces would pull out of the South and French forces out of the North.
■ There would be early elections in July 1956 to elect a government for the whole of Vietnam and reunite the country.

▼ **Source B** The domino theory. The cartoon shows US President Nixon on the left-hand side and Mao Zedong, the Chinese communist leader, on the right-hand side. It shows how, as the first domino, Cambodia, falls over to communism, it knocks over the others (which represent other countries in South-East Asia) to communism

The domino theory

US President Eisenhower believed in the 'domino theory' (see Source B and Source C).

He was determined to prevent the spread of communism to South Vietnam. He particularly feared that the joint elections, due to be held in July 1956, would lead to the election of Ho Chi Minh, whose popularity in the South had greatly increased since Dien Bien Phu (see Source D). Ho Chi Minh wanted a united, communist Vietnam. He was also supported by the Chinese. If South Vietnam became communist then it could be followed by Laos, Cambodia or other Asian countries.

> **Source C** Eisenhower explains the domino theory
>
> You have a row of dominoes set. You knock over the first one. What will happen to the last one is the certainty that it will go over very quickly. Asia has already lost some 450 million of its peoples to communist dictatorship. We simply can't afford greater losses.

> **Source D** Eisenhower writing, in later years, about the Vietnam War
>
> It was generally agreed that, had an election been held, Ho Chi Minh would have been elected Premier. Possibly 80 per cent of the population would have voted for the communist Ho Chi Minh as their leader.

Practice question

Give two things you can infer from Source C about the domino theory. (*For guidance, see page 79.*)

ACTIVITIES

1 What reason is suggested in Source D for US opposition to elections in Vietnam?

2 Summarise the following in not more than five words each:
   ■ Containment
   ■ The domino theory

Ngo Dinh Diem's election

Eisenhower was determined to maintain the government of South Vietnam. This meant propping up the president, Ngo Dinh Diem. Ngo Dinh Diem had served in the French administration of Vietnam in the 1930s. He emerged as a leader of South Vietnam in 1954. In October 1955 Diem was officially elected president of South Vietnam. However, the elections were rigged, with 605,000 people in Saigon voting for Diem despite Saigon only having a population of 450,000. The USA knew the elections were rigged but did nothing. They needed Diem as president. In addition, the USA had no intention of following the Geneva Agreement for a reunification election in 1956. They were certain that Ho Chi Minh would win. The July date for this election came and went. Diem, supported by the USA, refused to allow the election in South Vietnam. Diem knew that the USA would go on supporting him because he had prevented a communist victory in the South. The USA sent aid and military advisers to train the South Vietnamese army.

Weaknesses of the Diem government

Ngo Dinh Diem was not a popular or successful president. He was a Catholic while most Vietnamese were Buddhists. He packed his government with Roman Catholic landowners. He persecuted Buddhists, even going as far as banning the flying of the Buddhist flag on Buddha's birthday.

In June 1963, a 73-year-old Buddhist monk, Quang Duc, set himself alight as a protest against Diem's religious policy (see Source E). Madame Nhu, Diem's sister-in-law, responded by saying she hoped for more such 'barbecues'.

Diem's government was harsh, and he ruled as a dictator. He was only interested in hunting down supporters of the Vietminh and 're-educating' them in prison camps. Those who would not change their views were executed.

▲ **Source E** A Buddhist monk in 1963. This was one of several who burned themselves to death in protest against Diem's government

Eisenhower tried to encourage him to carry out land reform and give land to the peasants. However, Diem did quite the opposite. Land was taken from the peasants who were farming it at the time and given to Diem's supporters. The landowners forced their peasant tenants to pay high taxes and even made them work for nothing at certain times of the year. The few peasants who were given land had to pay for it in instalments. In total contrast to Diem, Ho Chi Minh carried out land reform and was a popular leader in North Vietnam. He would almost certainly have won the reunification election of 1956. His major aim was to reunite North Vietnam and South Vietnam under communist rule.

The growth of opposition

By the end of the 1950s, Diem's terror campaign had eliminated most of the Vietminh supporters in South Vietnam. In 1959 the communist government in the North issued orders to the Vietminh to begin a terror campaign against South Vietnamese officials. Over the next few years, an average of 4,000 officials a year were assassinated.

In 1960, former members of the Vietminh in South Vietnam, supported by Ho Chi Minh, set up the **National Liberation Front (NLF)** to oppose Diem's regime. It consisted of 12 different nationalist groups ranging from Buddhists to communists. The Front demanded the removal of Diem and land reform, and began a guerrilla campaign against the regime. The group consisted almost completely of South Vietnamese.

To Diem and the USA, all opposition was communist. The opposition was labelled the '**Vietcong**', a term of abuse that categorised all opponents as Vietnamese communists.

ACTIVITIES ?

The following are answers. Can you work out the questions?
- The NLF in 1960.
- It would have led to the election of Ho Chi Minh.
- He was a Buddhist monk who set himself alight.
- It meant that if one country fell to communism, it would quickly be followed by many others.

2 There were criticisms of US policy in Vietnam in the 1950s. How would Eisenhower and the US government have responded to the following criticisms?

Criticism	US response
The USA broke the Geneva Agreement	
The USA supported the corrupt Ngo Dinh Diem	
The USA opposed Ho Chi Minh	

9.3 Greater involvement under Kennedy

Within a few months of the formation of the NLF, John F. Kennedy became president of the USA.

Kennedy's aims

Kennedy was determined to get tough on communism and prevent its expansion in Asia. He decided to increase US involvement in Vietnam, to prop up the corrupt Diem regime and defeat the NLF and Vietcong. However, he was not, as yet, prepared to send combat troops. The US assistance included:

- increasing the number of military experts training the South Vietnamese Army, known as the Army of the Republic of Vietnam (ARVN). Over 16,000 advisers were sent during Kennedy's presidency, including the Army Special Forces known as the Green Berets
- equipping a further 20,000 troops for the ARVN, increasing it to 170,000.

In 1961 the USA spent $270 million in military support for Diem.

The overthrow of Diem

Kennedy realised that Diem was too unpopular to defeat the Vietcong. The US government gave its support to a plot by leading generals to overthrow Diem. On 1 November 1963, the troops supporting the *coup d'état* surrounded Diem's palace in Saigon. Diem appealed to the US Ambassador for help, but none was offered. The following day Diem was arrested and shot.

These US measures were too little too late. Diem's corrupt and unpopular government had greatly increased the support for the Vietcong. By the beginning of 1963 support for the Vietcong had increased to 23,000. Within a year and a half there were 170,000 Vietcong fighters. This was partly due to support from China. The increasing threat from the Vietcong was shown by the number of guerrilla attacks they carried out in the South, which increased from 50 to 150 between September and October of 1961. They won their first military victory against the South at Ấp Bắc in January 1963.

The governments that followed Diem were short-lived. The general who succeeded Diem lasted only three months. In January 1964 there was another *coup d'état* and the new military ruler, General Khanh, lasted one year.

ACTIVITIES ?

1 Why was Diem overthrown?
2 What was meant by the 'Strategic Hamlet' policy?
3 Why did the policy not work?

The Strategic Hamlet Program

The ARVN greatly outnumbered the Vietcong (VC) but, despite US aid, the ARVN was unable to defeat them. This was because of the VC's guerrilla tactics (see page 74) of attacking the ARVN and then disappearing into the jungle, and of the support of sympathetic villages in South Vietnam. In 1962, the USA developed a policy of creating strategic hamlets to provide greater security in the countryside. This involved moving peasants into fortified villages, guarded by troops. Nearly 3,000 strategic hamlets were set up, but the forced movement of peasants from their land and family burial sites caused much resentment. Indeed it brought even more support for the Vietcong.

The Strategic Hamlet policy meant that communist supporters were moved to a new area where they could spread their ideas. Those villagers who were not in the NLF often became supporters because of the way they were treated. As the situation worsened, Kennedy agreed to send more military support, including aircraft and intelligence equipment, as well as more advisers. Nevertheless he would still not send combat troops.

▲ John F. Kennedy was determined to stop communism spreading through Asia and sought to increase US involvement in Vietnam

9.4 Escalation of the conflict under President Johnson

When Kennedy was assassinated in November 1963 his successor, Lyndon Johnson, inherited a limited but growing US commitment to a war that was not going well for the USA. The Vietcong was becoming an increasing threat. There were nearly 60,000 guerrilla groups operating in South Vietnam by the end of 1964. They were being supplied by the Ho Chi Minh Trail, which ran from the North of Vietnam to the Vietcong in the south (see box below). Thirty-five per cent of South Vietnam was in Vietcong hands.

At first, Johnson did not want to extend US commitment to include combat troops. He preferred to expand the US advisory role. However, it soon became apparent that there would need to be much more direct US involvement to defeat the Vietcong. Johnson needed to convince **Congress** and the US public of the need for such commitment.

HO CHI MINH TRAIL

The Ho Chi Minh Trail was a supply line from the North of Vietnam to the Vietcong in the South. It ran through Laos and Cambodia in an attempt to avoid US bombing raids. The journey lasted about two months and was very dangerous, owing to the possibility of disease and attack. Nevertheless, it was the key to the success of the Vietcong as it ensured the replacement of troops and supplies.

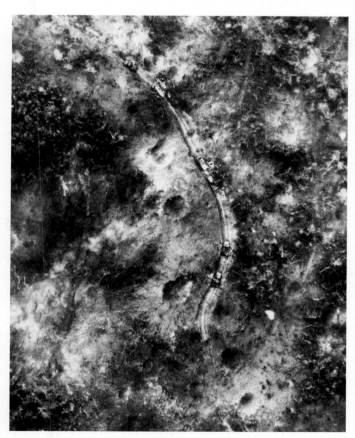

▲ **Source F** A view of the Ho Chi Minh Trail taken in 1966

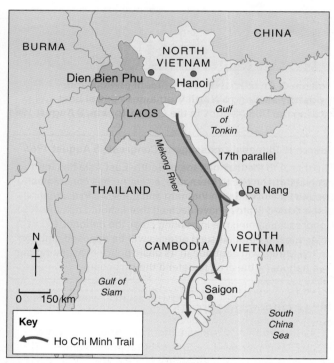

▲ **Figure 9.2** Map showing the Ho Chi Minh Trail and the Gulf of Tonkin

The Gulf of Tonkin incident, 1964

On 2 August 1964 the US destroyer *Maddox* was fired at by North Vietnamese patrol boats in the Gulf of Tonkin (see Source G). The *Maddox* was gathering intelligence information. Two days later there was a second alleged attack. Evidence later showed this did not happen. However, Johnson was able to use these attacks to persuade Congress to support greater US involvement in Vietnam (see Source H).

Congress believed that a second attack had taken place and that the North needed to be taught a lesson. It passed the Gulf of Tonkin Resolution that gave Johnson the power to take any military measures he thought necessary to defend South Vietnam.

▲ **Source G** An official US government photograph supposedly showing a North Vietnamese patrol boat attacking the USS *Maddox* in the Gulf of Tonkin, 2 August 1964

> **Source H** Johnson's message to Congress, 5 August 1964
>
> The threat to the free nations of South-East Asia has long been clear. The North Vietnamese regime has constantly tried to take over South Vietnam and Laos. As President of the United States I have decided that I should ask the Congress in joining me in making clear the national determination that all such attacks will be opposed, and the United States will continue in its basic policy of assisting the free nations of the area to defend their freedom.

Practice questions

1 Give **two** things you can infer from Source H about Johnson's motives for intervention in Vietnam.
(*For guidance, see page 79.*)

2 Explain why the US became involved in Vietnam in the years 1954–64.

You may use the following in your answer:
■ Domino theory
■ Gulf of Tonkin incident
You **must** also use information of your own.

(*For guidance, see pages 94–95.*)

▲ **Source I** The US destroyer *C Turner Joy* – the other warship supposedly attacked in the Gulf of Tonkin, 4 August 1964

Increased US involvement

Initially Johnson used the resolution to increase air support and attacks. However, in two battles, two élite battalions of South Vietnamese troops were defeated by Vietcong ambush tactics in 1964. United States air bases were also attacked by the NLF. In February 1965 the NLF guerrillas destroyed ten US helicopters, killed eight servicemen, and wounded over a hundred. In March 1965, 3,500 US combat troops arrived in Vietnam to protect US air bases. This number had increased to 200,000 by the end of the year and Johnson had launched 'Operation Rolling Thunder' (see page 76).

By 1968 President Johnson had increased the number of combat troops to half a million but the cost, both in dollars and in US casualties, was huge.

ACTIVITIES ?

1 The photograph in Source G was widely publicised by the US government. Devise a caption that they could have used for this photograph.

2 Make a copy of the table below showing possible reasons for US involvement in Vietnam in the 1950s and 1960s. Give each a rating of 1–5 for their importance (with 1 = unimportant to 5 = decisive). Give a brief explanation for each decision.

Reasons	Rating
Contain communism	
Defend democracy	
Extend US influence	

3 Create your own flow chart to show developments in Vietnam from 1939–64, indicating when and why the US became increasingly involved.

9.5 The utility question

This section provides guidance on how to answer the question about utility.

In answering the utility question, you must analyse various aspects of two sources and, in order to reach the top level, you need to cover them all. The content and nature, origin and purpose (NOP) of a source should be considered and out of this there will emerge an evaluation of the source's utility and reliability. In addition, you must also include knowledge of the historical context to support inferences and/or to assess the usefulness of information.

In order to reach higher level marks for this question you have to explain the value (usefulness) of both the content and the NOP of each source. The NOP is found in the provenance of the source – the information given above or below it. A good tip is to highlight or underline key words in the provenance which show the utility of the source. An example of this approach is given in Source A on page 72.

There is also guidance in the box below about what to consider for the NOP of a source.

NOP MEANS:

N Nature of the source

What type of source is it? A speech, a photograph, a cartoon, a letter, an extract from a diary? How will the nature of the source affect its utility? For example, a private letter is often very useful because the person who wrote it generally gives their honest views.

O Origins of the source

Who wrote or produced the source? Are their views worth knowing? Are they giving a one-sided view? When was it produced? It could be an eyewitness account. What are the advantages and disadvantages of eyewitness accounts?

P Purpose of the source

For what reason was the source produced? For example, the purpose of adverts is to make you buy the products. People usually make speeches to get your support. How will this affect the utility of the source?

Question 1

How useful is Source A for an enquiry into the reasons for US involvement in Vietnam? Explain your answer, using Source A and your knowledge of the historical context.

How to answer

Although in the exam the question will be on two sources, in Question 1 we only look at one source to help you build your skills in analysing a source. Question 2 on page 73 is about the utility of two sources.

First let us concentrate on content. For each source you should think about the following questions:

1   What is **useful** about the content of the source?

   ■   What does it mention? How useful is this compared to your own knowledge of the event? This is known as your contextual knowledge.

   ■   What view does it give about the feelings of people? Can you add any contextual knowledge to support your answer?

For example:

> Source A suggests that the USA feared the spread of communism in Vietnam and the threat to US ideology of freedom. This is useful because it provides evidence of one of the main reasons for US involvement in Vietnam – the domino theory – which believed that if one country fell in South-East Asia, such as Vietnam, it would soon be followed by others.

Now we will move on to NOP.

Page 72 shows examples of the values of the NOP of Source A as evidence of the reasons for US involvement in Vietnam.

Origins

It is useful because it is from a leading American and provides his motives for intervention in Vietnam. However, it is less useful because it is from a speech by a politician which was intended to draw support for his presidential campaign.

Source A From a speech given by John F. Kennedy during the campaign for the American presidency in 1960.

The enemy is the Communist system itself – relentless, impossible to satisfy, unceasing in its drive for world domination. This is not a struggle for supremacy of arms alone. It is also a struggle for supremacy between two ideologies: freedom under God versus ruthless, godless tyranny.

Nature

It is useful because it is from a speech by a leading American politician, who later became President and increased US involvement in Vietnam. However, it is less useful because the speech is written with the intention to persuade and may not be a typical US view of the time.

Purpose

It is useful because it provides the views given by leading politians in the USA in the early 1960s with the purpose of winning increased support for American involvement in Vietnam. It is less useful because it is quite general and does not specify which country is being threatened and by which enemy. Kennedy deliberately exaggerates the threat from communism in order to win support for his presidential campaign. Moreover, it may not reflect his genuine views but those of a politician on the election trail.

ACTIVITY

Now have a go answering Question 1 using all the guidance given on these two pages. Make a copy of the planning grid below and use it to plan your answer. Include the value and limitations of the contents of the source. Try to add some contextual knowledge when you make a point in the NOP columns.

	Value	Contextual knowledge
Contents		
What does the source tell you?		
What view does the source give?		
NOP		
Nature		
Origin		
Purpose		

The utility of two sources

For this paper you will need to evaluate the utility of two sources.

Question 2

How useful are Sources B and C for an enquiry into the reasons for US involvement in Vietnam? Explain your answer, using Sources B and C and your knowledge of the historical context.

> **Source B** From a speech by President Eisenhower to Congress, April 1954, just before the Geneva Conference on Vietnam
>
> Then with respect to more people passing under communist domination, Asia, after all, has already lost some 450 million of its peoples to the Communist dictatorship, and we simply can't afford greater losses. But when we come to the possible sequence of events, the loss of Indochina, of Burma, of Thailand, of the Peninsula, and Indonesia following, now you begin to talk about areas that not only multiply the disadvantages that you would suffer through the loss of materials, sources of materials, but now you are talking about millions and millions of people.

▲ **Source C** A cartoon which appeared in an American newspaper, *The Washington Star*, April 1965

How to answer

- Explain the value of the contents of each source and try to add some contextual knowledge when you make a point.
- Explain the value of the NOP of each source and try to add some contextual knowledge when you make a point.
- In your conclusion give a final judgement on the relative value of each source. For example, one source might provide one view of an event, the other source a different view.

Make a copy of the following grid to plan your answer for each source, and use the writing frame below.

Source B	Value	Contextual knowledge
Nature		
Origins		
Purpose		
Contents		

Below is a writing frame to help you:

> Source B is useful because it suggests (contents) _____
>
> Moreover Source B is also useful because of (NOP) _____
>
> This is supported by my contextual knowledge _____
>
> Source C is useful because (contents) it suggests _____
>
> This is supported by my contextual knowledge _____
>
> Moreover Source C is also useful because of (NOP) _____
>
> This is supported by my contextual knowledge _____

10 The nature of the conflict in Vietnam, 1964–68

The conflict in Vietnam became a struggle between two totally contrasting methods of warfare. The USA, the wealthiest nation in the world, used more conventional methods of warfare, in particular bombing and air support. This included the bombing of North Vietnam launched by Johnson in 1965, known as Operation Rolling Thunder. On the other side, North Vietnam and the Vietcong generally fought guerrilla warfare which included the very effective use of tunnels. The period 1964–68 culminated in the Tet Offensive of 1968, which was to have serious repercussions for both sides in the conflict.

10.1 The guerrilla tactics used by the Vietcong

The **Vietcong** mainly used guerrilla tactics to fight the war in the South. This was due to:

- the strength of US resources and equipment. The **North Vietnamese Army (NVA)** and Vietcong were no match for the USA and **ARVN** in open warfare
- support from the peasants in South Vietnam
- essential supplies from the North coming to the South via the Ho Chi Minh Trail (see page 69)
- their knowledge and understanding of the jungles of South Vietnam.

What were the guerrilla tactics?

Ho Chi Minh had studied the guerrilla tactics used by Mao Zedong in the 1930s and 1940s in his successful struggle against the Chinese Nationalist Party. Such tactics had been used against the Japanese during the Second World War and the French in the years that followed. Ho had learnt that the following simple principles worked:

- retreat when the enemy attacks
- raid when the enemy camps
- attack when the enemy tires
- pursue when the enemy retreats.

However, such tactics were dependent on the support of the local peasantry, who would be expected to hide the Vietcong. The Vietcong fighters were expected to be courteous and respectful to the villagers. Indeed they often helped the peasants in the fields during busy periods. This was in contrast to the tactics of 'Search and Destroy' (see page 77).

On the other hand, the Vietcong could be ruthless when necessary. They were prepared to kill peasants who opposed them or co-operated with their enemies. They also killed police, tax collectors, teachers and other employees of the government of South Vietnam. Between 1966 and 1971, the Vietcong killed an estimated 27,000 civilians.

How effective were guerrilla tactics?

The aim of the **guerrilla warfare** tactics was to wear down enemy soldiers and wreck their morale. This was very effective, as the US soldiers lived in constant fear of ambushes and booby traps. Indeed, 11 per cent of deaths were caused by booby traps. These were cheap and easy to make and very effective. Sharpened bamboo stakes, hidden in shallow pits under sticks and leaves, could easily pierce a boot.

The Vietcong were almost impossible to identify (see Source A). They did not wear uniforms and had no known base camp or headquarters. They worked in small groups and were hard to distinguish from the peasants in the villages. They attacked and then disappeared into the jungle, villages or tunnels.

> **Source A** Captain E. Banks, a US marine who fought in Vietnam, describes the difficulty in identifying the Vietcong
>
> You never knew who was an enemy and who was a friend. They all looked alike. They were all Vietnamese. Some of them were Vietcong. A woman says her husband isn't Vietcong. She watches your men walk down a trail and get killed by a booby trap. Maybe she planted it herself. The enemy was all around you.

> **Source B** One US soldier remembers the effects of a booby trap
>
> Pulaski tripped on a booby trap, and it blew the hell out of him. Evidently, the enemy stole the explosives or something. The explosion blew one leg off about midway between the knee and the groin, and the other leg was blown off at the calf. The explosion left his body naked.

The tunnels

The Vietcong feared US bombing raids. The communist forces dug deep tunnels and used them as air-raid shelters (Figure 10.1). For example, the tunnels around Saigon ran for 320 km. The tunnels were self-contained and booby-trapped and provided not only refuge from the bombing, but also a safe haven for the guerrilla fighters. They were also generally a death trap for US and ARVN forces.

Extensive tunnel systems had been used during the French Indo-China War, but when the Americans arrived, they were extended rapidly. Underground, the Vietcong had dormitories and workshops, hospitals, kitchens, headquarters facilities and supply depots.

Some tunnel systems ran for hundreds of miles, from the Cambodian border to the gates of Saigon itself. Short tunnels often looked as if they were dead ends when, in fact, a concealed trap door connected them to a vast network.

The tunnels were narrow, which suited the small Vietnamese soldiers but not the larger Americans. They were filled with booby traps, including rigged grenades, tethered poisonous snakes and sharpened bamboo stakes known as punji sticks.

▲ **Source C** A Vietnamese poster of 1968 showing the guerrilla warfare used by the Vietcong

ACTIVITY

Study Sources A, B, C and Figure 10.1. For each source, identify how they give evidence of guerilla tactics. You could put this in a table.

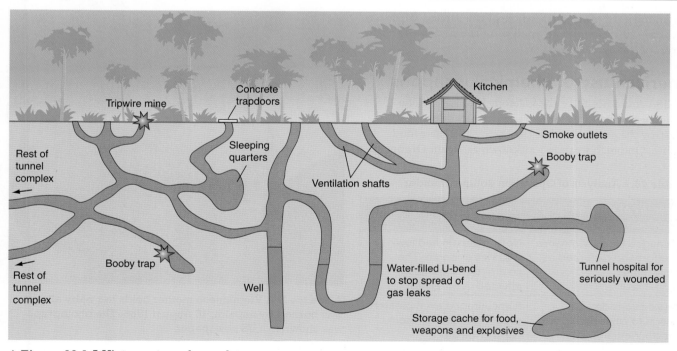

▲ **Figure 10.1 A Vietcong tunnel complex**

Practice questions

1   Give two things you can infer from Source B about the fighting in Vietnam. *(For guidance, see page 79.)*
2   How useful are Sources A and C as evidence of the reasons for US involvement in Vietnam? Explain your answer, using Sources A and C and your knowledge of the historical context. *(For guidance, see pages 71–73.)*

10.2 US methods of fighting the war

The methods used by the USA changed during the course of the 1960s, but were mainly based on:

- air power – this would enable them to destroy enemy supply lines and to equip their own forces in a **mobile war**
- their superiority in **artillery** and equipment – they realised that in most **pitched battles**, the superior US resources would prove decisive
- killing larger numbers of the enemy – the US commander in Vietnam, General Westmoreland, was convinced that 'a high enemy body count' would bring victory.

'Operation Rolling Thunder'

On 7 February 1965, the USA launched 'Operation Rolling Thunder'. This involved widespread bombing raids on military and industrial targets in North Vietnam. It was the beginning of an air offensive that was to last until 1968. Gradually the targets were extended to include cities in North and South Vietnam. The original intention was for an eight-week bombing offensive but it actually lasted for more than three and a half years. The USA dropped more bombs in Vietnam than were dropped by the Allies (the USA and Britain) during the whole of the Second World War. Table 10.1 provides an analysis of the successes and failures of the operation.

American use of chemical weapons

The USA could not force the Vietcong into battle. The decision was therefore made to use chemical weapons to destroy the jungle that hid the enemy and their food supplies. One such weapon was known as 'Agent Orange', a highly toxic weedkiller used to destroy the jungle – known as a defoliant. The Americans used 82 million litres of Agent Orange to spray thousands of square kilometres of jungle.

Napalm was another chemical weapon widely used by the USA. It was a type of bomb that exploded and showered the surrounding victims with a burning petroleum jelly. Napalm sticks to the skin and burns at 800 degrees centigrade. In other words, it burned through the skin to the bone.

These defoliants and chemical weapons had little effect in terms of flushing out the Vietcong. On the contrary, these methods increased support for the communists and made peasants more likely to hide Vietcong members.

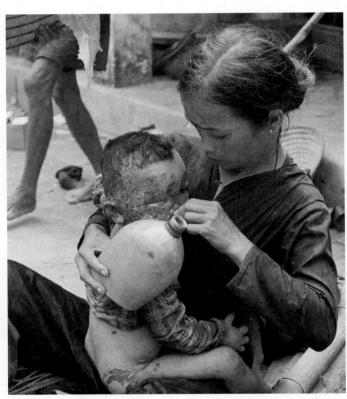

▲ **Source D** A Vietnamese mother holds her baby after it was burned by napalm, 16 August 1966. The photograph was shown in a US newspaper

▼ **Table 10.1** Analysis of Operation Rolling Thunder

Successes of the bombing campaign	Failures of the bombing campaign
It damaged North Vietnam's war effort and disrupted its supply routes	North Vietnam had few factories to bomb. The countryside was mostly affected
It caused considerable damage to cities and towns in North Vietnam	It encouraged even greater support for the war from North Vietnam
	It did not stop the supplies to the Vietcong from the North
	The cost was horrendous. In 1967 the US magazine, *Life*, calculated that it cost the USA $400,000 to kill one Vietcong fighter, a figure that included 75 bombs and 400 artillery shells

Source E A US pilot explains the effects of napalm bombing

The original napalm bomb wasn't so hot – if the **gooks** were quick they could scrape it off. So the boys started adding polystyrene – now it really sticks. But then if the gooks jumped in the water it stopped burning, so they started adding white phosphorus so as to make it burn better. It'll even burn under water now. And one drop is enough, it'll keep burning right down to the bone so they die anyway from phosphorus poisoning.

Tactics used on the ground

In 1964–65, the USA adopted a defensive strategy on the ground, using their first combat troops to defend their air bases. These troops patrolled up to a maximum of 80 km around the bases to ensure that there were no Vietcong (VC) in the area.

Johnson hoped that such a strategy would make the use of US troops in Vietnam more acceptable to the US public because there would be fewer casualties. Nevertheless, the US forces were determined to force the North Vietnamese Army (NVA) into a pitched battle where US superiority in equipment would be decisive. In November 1965, for example, US forces fought their first battle against NVA forces in the La Drang Valley. The NVA lost about 1,800 men, while the USA had 240 casualties. However, this was not a total victory for the US forces for the following reasons:

- The NVA retreated into neutral Cambodia and the US forces could not follow.
- The 'body count' seemed to favour the USA and Westmoreland was convinced that the North Vietnamese would not be able to survive such casualties. He was wrong. The communists were so committed to their cause that they would accept these losses. The US public, however, did not accept their much smaller losses.

Within a few months Johnson gave Westmoreland permission to adopt more aggressive tactics, known as 'Search and Destroy'. Interestingly, the president did not inform the US public.

'Search and Destroy'

Westmoreland established secure and heavily defended US bases in the south of the country near the coast. From here, US and ARVN forces launched 'Search and Destroy' tactics using helicopters. They would descend on a village suspected of assisting the Vietcong forces and destroy it. The troops called these attacks 'Zippo' raids after the name of the cigarette lighters they used to set fire to the thatched houses of the villages. These raids would kill a number of Vietcong guerrilla fighters, but:

- inexperienced US troops often walked into traps
- incorrect information often meant that innocent villages were destroyed

- this, in turn, made the USA and ARVN very unpopular with many South Vietnamese peasants who were then more likely to support the Vietcong
- civilian casualties were often very high, with most having little or no connection with the Vietcong.

> **Source F** From an article by US journalist Neil Sheehan. It includes an account by Doug Ramsey of what happened to a village when he was working for the Agency for International Development (AID) in Vietnam
>
> The rubble of the hamlet was still smoking, and it was obvious that these people had returned only a short time before to discover what had happened to their homes. Children were whimpering. Women were poking through the smouldering debris of the houses trying to save cooking utensils and other small possessions that might have escaped the flames. The soldiers had even burned all of the rice that had not been buried or hidden elsewhere. A middle-aged farmer in the group asked Ramsey what agency he worked for. 'AID', Ramsey replied. 'AID', the farmer cried. 'Look about you', he said whilst pointing at the charred ruins of the village. 'Here is your American AID'! The farmer spat on the ground and walked away.

▲ **Source G** US soldiers destroying a village suspected of supporting the Vietcong

Practice question

Explain why there was criticism of the tactics used by the USA in Vietnam.

You may use the following in your answer:
- Use of chemical weapons
- Search and Destroy

You **must** also use information of your own.

(For guidance, see pages 94–95.)

ACTIVITIES ❓

1 What can you learn from Sources D and E (page 76) about the effects of napalm?

2 What can you learn from Source F about the effects of the US 'Search and Destroy' tactics?

3 Using Sources F and G and your own knowledge, explain why the 'Search and Destroy' tactics failed.

4 The USA failed to deal with the guerrilla tactics used by the Vietcong. Can you suggest any change of strategy to better deal with these tactics?

10.3 The Tet Offensive, 1968

On 31 January 1968, the Vietcong launched a massive attack on over 100 cities and towns in the South during the New Year, or Tet, holiday. It was launched by the Vietcong for several reasons:

- The Vietcong knew this was a public holiday and half the ARVN were on leave.
- They were aware that the war was unpopular in the USA. Public opinion would not welcome a US defeat in South Vietnam and so this might force them out of the conflict.
- At best, the USA would need reinforcements to force the Vietcong out of the cities and towns. US public opinion might prevent the dispatch of extra troops.
- The Vietcong hoped that their offensive would inspire mass support from the people of South Vietnam.

The Vietcong made rapid advances into many major towns and cities and other military targets. The most dramatic event was when a fifteen-man suicide squad of Vietcong guerrillas fought their way into the US Embassy in Saigon (see Source J). They held out for five hours until it was recaptured. The whole event was shown live on US television. In Saigon, 4,500 Vietcong fighters kept a much larger US and ARVN force occupied for two days.

The Vietcong also captured the major northern city of Hué. They held it for 25 days before it was recaptured by the US and ARVN forces. However, while in Hué, the Vietcong executed anyone suspected of collaborating with the USA or the South Vietnamese government. Possibly as many as 3,000 people were killed.

The Tet Offensive proved an important turning point in the conflict as it showed that the Vietcong could strike at the heart of the American-held territory, especially the capture of the US Embassy in Saigon. It brought a further loss of US military morale (see Source H) and suggested to the US public that the war was unwinnable.

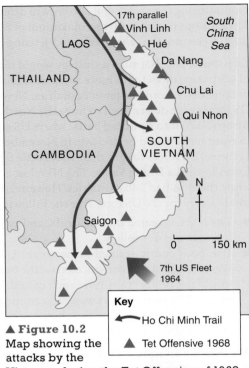

▲ **Figure 10.2**
Map showing the attacks by the Vietcong during the Tet Offensive of 1968

Source H From as interview given by Huong Van Ba, an artillery officer in the NVA, to an American interviewer, about the Tet Offensive

When the Tet campaign was over, we didn't have enough men left to fight a major battle, only to make hit-and-run attacks on posts. So many men had been killed that morale was very low. We spent a great deal of time hiding in tunnels, trying to avoid being captured. We experienced desertions and many of our men filtered back to their homes to join local guerrilla forces instead of staying with the main NVA units. We heard that in the North there were more young people trying to avoid the draft.

ACTIVITIES

1 Organise the statements shown in Figure 10.3 about the results of the battle into two categories: 'Success for the South' and 'Success of the North'.

2 Overall, who do you think gained most from the Tet Offensive? Give a brief explanation of your answer.

The Vietcong lost most of its fighters and its independence. It was now more closely controlled by Hanoi.

The offensive destroyed many of the finest Vietcong fighters.

US casualties only came to 1,500.

The US public were shocked by the attack on the embassy.

In military terms it was a disaster for the Vietcong. Most of the 4,500 fighters were killed.

The ancient city of Hué was destroyed.

AVRN casualties were 3,000.

Very few people in the South joined the Vietcong offensive.

Many people in the USA, having seen the Vietcong reach the US embassy, were now convinced that the war could not be won.

The USA and AVRN had to use a lot of artillery and air power to defeat the Vietcong.

▲ **Figure 10.3** Results of the Tet Offensive

10.4 Inference question

This section provides guidance on how to answer the source inference question.

Question 1

Give two things you can learn from Source A about the Tet Offensive. **(4 marks)**

> **Source A** From an interview given by Huong Van Ba, an artillery officer in the NVA, to an American interviewer, about the Tet Offensive.
>
> When the Tet campaign was over, we didn't have enough men left to fight a major battle, only to make hit-and-run attacks on posts. So many men had been killed that morale was very low. We spent a great deal of time hiding in tunnels, trying to avoid being captured. We experienced desertions and many of our men filtered back to their homes to join local guerrilla forces instead of staying with the main NVA units. We heard that in the North there were more young people trying to avoid the draft.

How to answer

This is an inference question.

- You are being asked to give the message or messages of the source, to read between the lines of what is written.
- In addition, you must support the inference. In other words, use details from the source to support the messages you say it gives.
- Begin your answer with 'This source suggests …'
  This should help you get messages from the source.
- Aim for two supported inferences to be sure of full marks.
  For example, in Source A two messages could be:

Question 2

Give two things you can learn from Source A about guerrilla warfare in Vietnam. **(4 marks)**

> **Source B** Captain E. Banks, a US marine who fought in Vietnam, describes the difficulty in identifying the Vietcong
>
> You never knew who was an enemy and who was a friend. They all looked alike. They were all Vietnamese. Some of them were Vietcong. A woman says her husband isn't Vietcong. She watches your men walk down a trail and get killed by a booby trap. Maybe she planted it herself. The enemy was all around you.

> **ACTIVITY** ?
>
> Now have a go answering Question 2 using the steps shown for Question 1.

Inference
Source A suggests that the Tet Offensive was a failure for the Vietcong.

Support from the source
I know this because the source says that so many men had been killed and others were having to hide in tunnels.

Source A
When the Tet campaign was over, we didn't have enough men left to fight a major battle, only to make hit-and-run attacks on posts. So many men had been killed that morale was very low. We spent a great deal of time hiding in tunnels, trying to avoid being captured. We experienced desertions and many of our men filtered back to their homes to join local guerrilla forces instead of staying with the main NVA units. We heard that in the North there were more young people trying to avoid the draft.

Inference
Source A suggests that the Tet Offensive greatly reduced enthusiasm for the war in the North.

Support from the source
I know this because the source says that in the North many young men were trying to avoid the draft.

American policy in Vietnam changed under Nixon, who was elected president in 1968. Nixon introduced a policy of Vietnamisation which involved the withdrawal of American troops from Vietnam, but he also escalated the war, with attacks on Cambodia and Laos. This escalation led to even greater opposition to the war by the American people and convinced Nixon that he had to end the involvement of the USA in Vietnam as soon as possible. Peace talks, which had begun as early as 1969, brought about a peace settlement in 1973.

11.1 Nixon's policies

By 1969, more than 36,000 members of the US military had been killed in the war. In May of that year, President Nixon unveiled his plan to end US involvement. This policy was known as Vietnamisation.

Vietnamisation

The purpose behind Vietnamisation was to enable the USA to withdraw troops from Vietnam by getting the South Vietnamese to take on much more responsibility for the war. Nixon announced the first withdrawal of 25,000 US troops in June 1969, followed by 60,000 six months later.

The idea was that South Vietnamese soldiers would be trained and equipped to take the place of US troops. As the South Vietnamese took over more of the fighting, US troops would begin to return home. President Thieu's government in the South would still be given financial and military aid and the US air force would continue to support ground troops.

It was introduced in order to fulfill Nixon's election promises to end the war in Vietnam as well as due to the increasing opposition to the war in the USA (see pages 85–90).

Reasons for its failure

The Vietnamisation strategy did not work. The Hanoi government realised that the anti-war movement in the USA would eventually force an American withdrawal, leaving the South to fight alone. Moreover, the ARVN would be no match for the communist forces. South Vietnam would be reunited with the North. Even senior US military commanders in South Vietnam believed that the ARVN would, at best, only be able to contain the forces of the North once US military support had been withdrawn. Nevertheless, Nixon continued to back this policy throughout the autumn of 1969 (see Source A.)

Source A From President Nixon's television speech, 3 November 1969

My fellow Americans ... we have only two choices if we want to end this war. I can order an immediate withdrawal of all US troops without regard to the effects of that action. Or we can persist in our search for a just peace through a negotiated settlement if possible through the continued implementation of our plan for Vietnamisation.

I have chosen the second course. It is not the easy way. It is the right way. It is a plan which will end the war and serve the course of peace. And so tonight, the great silent majority of my fellow Americans, I ask for your support.

▲ **Source B** A cartoon about the US policy of Vietnamisation

The madman theory

Nixon's advisers told him that they feared that the gradual removal of all US troops would eventually result in a National Liberation Front victory. It was therefore agreed that the only way that the USA could avoid a humiliating defeat was to negotiate a peace agreement in the talks that were taking place in Paris. Here the Americans used the madman theory in an attempt to scare the Hanoi government into accepting peace terms with due speed (see Source C). The madman theory was simple – it was an attempt to convince the government in Hanoi that Nixon so hated communism and was so taken in by the domino theory (see page 66) that he was planning to use nuclear weapons against North Vietnam if the war continued. Clearly such a ploy did not upset the North Vietnamese representatives as the Paris talks went on for some time (see pages 97–98).

> **Source C** Here Nixon is speaking to one of his chief aides Bob Haldeman, who attended the peace talks in 1969
>
> I call it the madman theory, Bob. I want the North Vietnamese to believe I've reached the point where I might do anything to stop the war. We'll just slip the word – 'Nixon is obsessed about communism. We can't restrain him when he's angry and he has his hand on the nuclear button' – and then Ho Chi Minh himself will be in Paris in two days begging for peace.

The Nixon Doctrine

Nixon also announced the Nixon Doctrine, in which he proclaimed that the USA would honour its current defence commitments but that it would not commit troops anywhere else.

> **ACTIVITY** ?
>
> What is the message of Sources B and D?

Practice questions

1 Give **two** things you can infer from Source A about Nixon's policy in Vietnam. (*For guidance, see page 79.*)
2 How useful are Sources A and C for an enquiry into Nixon's policies towards the war? Explain your answer, using Sources A and C and your knowledge of the historical context. (*For guidance, see pages 71–73.*)

▼ **Source D** A cartoon commenting on Nixon's war policy

11.2 The war spreads

Nixon's policy of Vietnamisation had one very important consequence. It led to US involvement in Cambodia and Laos.

Attacks on Cambodia, 1970 and Laos, 1971

Nixon ordered the bombing of Cambodia because the **Vietcong** and **NVA** were using safe havens there as springboards for offensives into South Vietnam. The Ho Chi Minh Trail (see page 69) was extensively bombed. Although Cambodia was officially a neutral nation, the NVA had long used its territory to run weapons and troops, circumventing the US soldiers, bombers and raiding parties that were operating in Vietnamese territory. In the spring of 1970, Nixon authorised a series of bombing raids in Cambodia and sent both US and **ARVN** troops across the border, all without the consent, or even the awareness, of **Congress**.

The Cambodian campaign sent shock waves through Congress and the US public. The Americans dropped close to 3 million tons of bombs on Cambodia. There are no official figures of the number of deaths caused by the bombing but most experts believe that as many as 100,000 were killed and as many as 2 million were made homeless. There was renewed public outcry and waves of demonstrations at colleges and universities across the USA as the media published details of the bombings. Despite continuing protest, Nixon called on the '**silent majority**' to support him. Polls did seem to indicate that a majority of US citizens agreed with his policy.

The war continued to broaden in February 1971, when South Vietnamese troops, with US air support, invaded Laos. Five thousand élite South Vietnamese troops were sent to destroy parts of the Ho Chi Minh Trail. The troops met groups of the North Vietnamese Army, which was well equipped with Soviet weapons, and were soundly defeated. At least half of their force was killed.

> **Source E** From a speech by President Nixon, 30 April 1970. He was explaining his decision to send troops to Cambodia
>
> The action I have taken is completely necessary for the success of the withdrawal program from Vietnam. A majority of the American people want to keep the casualties of our brave men in Vietnam at an absolute minimum. The invasion of Cambodia is essential if we are to achieve that goal. We take this action for the purpose of ending this war.

> **Source F** From an article in the newspaper, St. Louis Post-Dispatch, on 3 May 1970
>
> In asking the American people to support the expansion of the Vietnam War to Cambodia, they are asked to seek peace by making war, seek withdrawal of our troops by enlarging the arena of combat and to diminish US casualties by sending more young men to their death.

> **Source G** From the recollections of Ken Craig, a naval aviator, who flew over Laos on many missions
>
> I think whoever dreamed up that one, I mean, it could've been doable but they got to look at the terrain. That terrain is the most difficult in the world. You're not going to easily send even a battalion-sized group of people into the middle of Laos and do anything significant. The terrain is very difficult and you can lose a thousand people in the jungle.

ACTIVITIES ?

1 Working in pairs, look at Sources A (see page 80), E, F and G. Do you think that President Nixon was justified in extending the war into Cambodia and Laos?

2 Copy the table below and then construct your case, explaining your reasons.

Nixon was justified	Nixon was not justified

The bombing of North Vietnam

In order to prevent the communists from making too many gains, Nixon had to rely on the US air force to bomb the enemy. There were increased air raids after 1971, and B52 bombers attacked the North for the first time since 1967. When peace talks stumbled in early autumn 1972, Nixon was enraged.

In October 1972, Henry Kissinger, the US Secretary of State, announced that 'peace was at hand', but when President Thieu refused to accept the terms (see page 97), Nixon decided to escalate the bombing. Bombing began on 18 December and continued for 12 days (except on Christmas Day). The operation was called 'Operation Linebacker II' – an attack aimed at winning concessions from the communists at peace talks in Paris. The campaign, coming shortly after Nixon had won a landslide election to a second presidential term, was the biggest aerial attack of the war. In Hanoi and the northern port city of Haiphong, the bombing was relentless. More than 1,600 civilians died and 70 US airmen were killed or captured. The *New York Times* called the bombing 'Diplomacy through terror'.

▲ **Source H** The effects of the US bombing of Hanoi, Christmas 1972

ACTIVITY

1 Working in pairs, devise two different captions for Source H:
   a) The first if it was published in a US newspaper
   b) The other if it was published in a North Vietnamese newspaper.

Practice questions

Explain why there was criticism of Nixon's policies in Vietnam.

> You may use the following in your answer:
> ■ Vietnamisation
> ■ Bombing of Cambodia
> You **must** also use information of your own.

(For guidance, see pages 94–95.)

Reactions to, and the end of, US involvement in Vietnam, 1964–75

This key topic examines the reactions to the war in the USA. There was a significant number of Americans who, at least at first, supported the war, mainly because of the fear of the spread of communism to South-East Asia. However, a growing number also opposed the war, more especially as the number of American casualties increased. This opposition was to play an important role in influencing the policies of both Johnson and Nixon.

Each chapter within this key topic explains a key issue and examines important lines of enquiry as outlined below.

There will also be guidance on how to answer the causation question (pages 94–95).

CHAPTER 12 ATTITUDES TO THE WAR IN THE USA

- Reasons for the growth of opposition, including the student movement, TV and media coverage of the war and the draft system.
- Public reaction to the My Lai Massacre, 1968. The trial of Lieutenant Calley. The Kent State University shootings, 1970.
- Reasons for early support for the war, including the fear of communism.
- The 'hard hats' and the 'silent majority'.

CHAPTER 13 THE PEACE PROCESS AND END OF THE WAR

- Reasons for, and features of, the peace negotiations, 1972–73.
- The significance of the Paris Peace Agreement, 1973.
- The economic and human costs of the war for the USA.

CHAPTER 14 REASONS FOR THE FAILURE OF THE USA IN VIETNAM

- The strengths of the North Vietnam, including the significance of Russian and Chinese support, Vietcong tactics and the Ho Chi Minh Trail.
- The weaknesses of the US armed forces. The failure of US tactics.
- The impact of opposition to the war in the USA.

TIMELINE 1968–75

1968	Johnson decides not to stand for re-election as president. The My Lai Massacre	1972	Nixon's visit to China. The October Agreement
1969	Nixon begins secret peace talks with North Vietnam	1973	Ceasefire agreed. Paris Peace Agreement signed
1970	The Kent State University shootings	1975	Vietnam reunited

12 Attitudes to the war in the USA

Opposition to the war in the USA emerged in the mid and late 1960s. It grew stronger owing to television coverage of the war and the increase in US casualties. Many young people, fearful of the draft, joined the anti-war movement and took part in the increasing number of protest marches and rallies. Government reaction to these protests culminated in the Kent State University shootings of 1970. This opposition certainly contributed to the eventual withdrawal of the USA from the conflict in Vietnam, as well as President Johnson's decision not to seek re-election in 1968. However, a significant number of Americans did support the war.

12.1 Opposition to the war

For the duration of the Vietnam War, successive US governments tried to make the public believe that opposition was mainly from young students who had 'dropped out' of society. This was an attempt to discredit those opposed to the war. Although some of the protesters were students, there was opposition from different sectors of US society, for a variety of reasons including:

- politicians who were against any involvement in Vietnam because of the corrupt nature of the regime in South Vietnam
- returning US troops who had experienced the horrors of the war
- black Americans who felt that attaining civil rights for themselves in the USA was more important than the war. Black Americans also suffered from government economic cutbacks caused by the expense of the war
- women of all backgrounds – young, old, black and white. Indeed, the Women's International League for Peace and Freedom was one of the first to protest.

Some groups were influenced by the general protest movement of the time in the USA and others by events in Vietnam itself.

▼ Source A An image shown on US television in 1967 showing dead and wounded soldiers after a Vietcong attack. Television coverage made opposition to the war grow

Protest in the USA

The 1960s saw the emergence of several protest movements that were already well established before the USA became involved in Vietnam, as shown in Figure 12.1.

Civil rights movement

This was the movement for equal rights for black US citizens led by Martin Luther King (**see Source B**). It had a lot of support from young black and white students. The civil rights movement used a whole range of methods to achieve its aims, including marches and sit-ins. Protesters against Vietnam later adopted these same methods in their demonstrations.

The anti-war movement also won support from the civil rights movement and many black youths. This was because the proportion of blacks conscripted into the Vietnam War was much higher than that of the white population. This was seen as another example of the racist policies of the US government. A high profile opponent of the draft was Muhammad Ali, the heavyweight boxing champion of the world, who was stripped of his title for refusing to fight in Vietnam. He said: 'I'm a black person, the Vietnamese are brown people. We do not have anything against each other.'

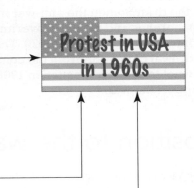

The student movement

Many young Americans were unhappy with the older generation and thought they were out of touch with the issues of the day. Students started to protest against the government for changes, such as better rights for black citizens. A lot of young students felt that the Vietnam War was another example of the government's abuse of power and wanted to make a stand against the conflict (see Sources C and D).

Protest singers, such as Bob Dylan, became very popular with students, who saw these artists as expressing their own views about society at that time. Indeed one of Dylan's most famous songs, Blowin' in the Wind, was about the hypocrisy of war.

The 'Great Society'

Some people opposed the war because the conflict undermined President Johnson's attempts to improve the country through what he called the 'Great Society' – a series of reforms designed to reduce unemployment and improve medical services and education. However, they were not fully carried out, as resources were diverted to the war in Vietnam (see Source E). The war was costing $20 billion a year and the concept of the 'Great Society' was pushed to one side.

▲ **Figure 12.1** Protest in 1960s USA

Source B Martin Luther King speaking against the war, 1967

We were taking the young black men who had been ruined by our society and sending them 8,000 miles away to defend freedom in South-East Asia – a freedom which they had not found in their own country, in places like South-West Georgia and East Harlem. Instead, we have repeatedly seen the cruel image of Negro and white boys on TV screens as they kill and die together for a nation that has been unable to provide schools in which Negro and white children can sit together.

Source C A student slogan against the war in Vietnam

Hey! Hey! LBJ [Lyndon B. Johnson]

How many kids did you kill today?

We don't want your war

Draft beer, not boys

Dump Johnson

Eighteen today, dead tomorrow

▲ **Source D** A student demonstration at the University of California, Berkeley, in 1967

▲ **Source E** A cartoon in a British magazine in 1967. It shows President Johnson breaking up the 'Great Society'

ACTIVITIES

1 What can you learn from Sources B and C about attitudes in the USA to the war in Vietnam?

2 What message is the cartoonist trying to get across in Source E?

3 Using Sources F and G (page 88) explain how the media influenced attitudes to the war.

Practice questions

1 Give two things you can infer from Source C about opposition to the War in Vietnam. (*For guidance, see page 79.*)

2 How useful are Sources C and E for an enquiry into the opposition to US involvement in the war in Vietnam? Explain your answer, using Sources C and E and your knowledge of the historical context. (*For guidance, see pages 71–73.*)

Reasons for the growth of opposition

There were several reasons for the growing opposition to US involvement in the war in Vietnam and these are outlined below Figure 12.2 (page 88) also shows how public opposition to the war in Vietnam increased over time.

Political

Some people questioned the reasoning behind the US involvement in Vietnam. The US Government suggested it was a war to protect democracy and freedom against the spread of communism. Yet Diem's regime in South Vietnam was corrupt, undemocratic and unpopular. The USA seemed to be fighting to prop up a military dictatorship.

The Pentagon Papers of 1971 increased this political opposition. These were a collection of government documents relating to the war in Vietnam. They were leaked to the media and published by the *New York Times*. They showed how confused the government was over the war and how they had deliberately lied to the public.

US casualties

Opposition to the war grew with the number of US casualties. In 1965 there were fewer than 2,000 US casualties but this had increased to 14,000 by 1968. Indeed, in 1967, ex-soldiers formed Vietnam Veterans Against the War, stating that the war was not worth the casualties.

Media coverage of the war

Television and photography also greatly influenced public opinion. The war in Vietnam was the first to be televised in great detail. Moreover, in the mid and late 1960s, colour television became readily accessible, which worsened the bloody nature of what was shown. The conflict was in the living rooms of most US families. This, together with photographs, revealed the brutality of the conflict and showed the appalling injuries caused by the use of **napalm** on civilians, including children (see Source G, page 88). In addition, television seemed to show that the USA had little hope of winning the conflict.

Source F General Westmoreland, who commanded the US forces in Vietnam until 1968, gave his views on the US media in 1979

Actions by opponents of the war in the United States were supported by the news media. The media, no doubt, helped to back up the message that the war was 'illegal' and 'immoral'. Then came the enemy's Tet Offensive of early 1968. The North Vietnamese and Vietcong suffered a military defeat. Despite this, reporting of the offensive by the press and television in the USA gave the impression of an endless war that could never be won.

US methods of warfare

The methods of warfare used by the USA also brought much opposition:

- Chemical warfare angered environmentalists because of the damage it did to the jungle in Vietnam, as well as to civilians.
- The US public saw bombing from the air as brutal and unnecessary.
- Many were appalled by the suffering caused by 'Search and Destroy' missions (see page 77).

▲ **Source G** A woman holding a baby severely burned by napalm. Such images increased opposition to the war in Vietnam

The draft system

Anti-war protestors launched a campaign against the conscription of young men into the army. Conscription had existed since the Second World War. However, there were exemptions to the system that seemed to favour the wealthy middle class. A much higher proportion of black and working-class Americans seemed to be called up.

The Draft Resistance Movement was formed, giving advice on how to avoid conscription. Other protestors burnt their draft cards. By the end of 1969 there were 34,000 draft dodgers wanted by the police. Many crossed the border into Canada to avoid arrest. A quarter of a million men avoided conscription.

Other groups raided draft board offices and burnt their records. At first those who took part were harshly punished with as much as six years in prison. However, the sentences got shorter as the protest (and the war) went on.

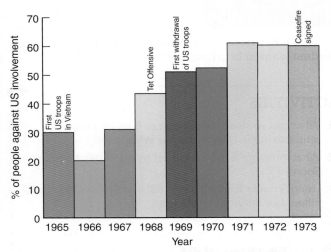

▲ **Figure 12.2** A graph showing the US public's opposition to the war in Vietnam, 1965–73

Practice question

Give **two** things you can infer from Figure 12.2 about opposition to the war. (*For guidance, see page 79.*)

Public reaction to the My Lai Massacre, 1968

The My Lai Massacre on 16 March 1968 caused public outrage. A US patrol was carrying out a 'Search and Destroy' mission just south of Khe Sanh during the Tet Offensive. Lieutenant Calley and his platoon wiped out the village of My Lai, killing at least 347 men, women, children and babies. Some of the women had been raped first.

The US military tried to keep news of the massacre quiet. Indeed they even boasted of its success in killing 90 Vietcong fighters. However, a year and a half later, in November 1969, the US press got hold of the story from a soldier who had heard about the massacre. *Life* magazine published details of the massacre and this sparked off an official investigation.

The trial of Lt Calley

Calley and ten other officers were formally charged with murdering 109 people. The charges were too much for the army. They placed all the responsibility on Calley who was the only one found guilty and was given 20 years of hard labour in 1971. He was released in 1974.

> **Source H** Seymour Hersh was the US journalist who revealed the massacre. He describes some of the events of the massacre using evidence from the villagers themselves
>
> Le Tong, a 28-year-old rice farmer, reported seeing one woman raped after GIs killed her children. Nguyen Khoa, a 37-year-old peasant, told of a 13-year-old girl who was raped before being killed. GIs then attacked Khoa's wife, tearing her clothes off. Before they could rape her, however, Khoa said, their six-year-old son, riddled with bullets, fell and saturated her with blood. The GIs left her alone.

▲ **Source I** Civilians of My Lai, killed by US soldiers

My Lai shocked US public opinion. It was the clearest evidence that the war was going wrong. In November 1969, more than half a million anti-war protesters demonstrated in Washington, DC. It was the largest political protest in American history. However, a large number of Americans either refused to believe the massacre had happened or felt it was justified because the villagers were helping the Vietcong.

Operation Phoenix

'Operation Phoenix' brought further opposition to the war. In 1968 the US Central Intelligence Agency (CIA) set up 'Operation Phoenix'. The aim was to identify and arrest at least 3,000 Vietcong suspects each month. They were to be arrested and forced to reveal the names of other Vietcong. In total they arrested 28,000 suspects, many of whom were tortured. Although many were Vietcong, a number were innocent. The US public were distinctly uncomfortable with such brutal methods (see Source J).

> **Source J** A CIA officer gave evidence before Congress in 1968 about the methods used in 'Operation Phoenix'
>
> A six-inch piece of wood was inserted into one of my prisoner's ears and then tapped through the brain until he died. The starving to death in a cage of a Vietnamese woman who was suspected of being a part of the local VC political education group in one of the local villages ... The use of electronic gear such as sealed telephones attached to the men's testicles to shock them into giving information ...

ACTIVITIES

1 Study Sources H and I. Why would these have shocked many people in the USA?

2 Working in pairs, pretend you are US journalists reporting on the My Lai massacre. Using Sources H and I and the text on this page:
   a) Put together a front page headline for a US newspaper about the massacre.
   b) Describe the My Lai Massacre.
   c) Give your views on the massacre.

3 Working in pairs, put together two one-minute news items for US television based on Sources A (page 85) and H.

4 Why might Source J encourage further opposition to the war?

5 Describe two features of the growth of opposition to US involvement in the war Vietnam.

The Kent State University shootings, 1970

In the autumn of 1969 there were large demonstrations against the war. These protests grew worse when, in 1970, Nixon ordered the invasion of Cambodia (see page 82). He insisted this was only to destroy communist bases used by the Vietcong. College students organised another round of protests. Moreover, many were incensed by a speech he made in May 1970 (see Source K).

National Guardsmen were called to disperse students protesting at Kent State University, and used tear gas to try to move them. When the students refused to move shots were fired. Four people were killed and eleven injured (see Source M). The press in the USA and abroad were horrified, and some 400 colleges were closed as 2 million students went on strike in protest against this action. A few days later two students at another university who were protesting against the killings at Kent State University were shot dead by police.

> **Source K** Part of Nixon's speech, 1 May 1970
>
> You think of those kids out there (in Vietnam). They are the greatest. You see these bums blowing up the campuses … they are the luckiest people in the world, going to the greatest universities and here they are burning up the books, I mean storming around about – get rid of the war. Out there [in Vietnam] we've got kids who are just doing their duty. They stand tall and they are proud.

> **Source L** Arthur Krause, the father of one of the students who died at Kent State University, talking about his daughter on TV, 5 May 1970
>
> She resented being called a bum because she disagreed with someone else's opinion. She felt that our crossing into Cambodia was wrong. Is this dissent a crime? Is this a reason for killing her? Have we come to such a state in this country that a young girl has to be shot because she disagrees deeply with the action of her government?

▲ **Source M** The front page of the *Daily Mirror* showing one of the students killed at Kent State University. Those who supported the war called students 'campus bums'

ACTIVITIES

1 Write an imaginary headline for a US national newspaper the day after the Kent State University deaths.

2 Match the sentences in column A to the sentences in column B. The series of sentences will produce a summary of the anti-war movement.

A	B
The anti-war movement began during the presidency of Johnson.	This led to a further round of student protests.
In 1970 Nixon ordered the invasion of Cambodia.	At this meeting National Guardsmen panicked when faced with student protestors and killed four students.
One such student meeting took place at Kent State University.	It gave advice on how to avoid conscription.
The Draft Resistance Movement was set up.	Students organised sit-ins and protests.

Practice questions

1 Give two things you can infer from Source K about Nixon's attitude to those who opposed the war in Vietnam. (*For guidance, see page 79.*)

2 How useful are Sources L and M for an enquiry into the Kent State University shootings? Explain your answer, using Sources L and M and your knowledge of the historical context. (*For guidance, see pages 71–73.*)

12.2 Support for the war

Those that opposed the war in Vietnam received much publicity. However, there was a significant number who supported the war.

Reasons for support

In 1964, 85 per cent of Americans supported the government policy in the war. Even as late as 1970, after the invasion of Cambodia, a Gallup opinion poll showed 50 per cent approved of the invasion and only 35 per cent opposed it.

There were a number of active and enthusiastic supporters of the war who were concerned about the spread of communism in Asia. The fear of communism in the USA had increased after the Second World War, especially with Soviet expansion in Eastern Europe, the victory of Mao and the Communists in the Chinese Civil War, and the Korean War of 1950–53 in which the USA intervened to support South Korea against invasion from the Communist North. Moreover, the USA had experienced a **Red Scare** of the later 1940s and early 1950s encouraged by the activities of the Republican **senator**, Joe McCarthy. McCarthy insisted that Communist spies were everywhere but more especially in the State Department of government.

The activities of the Vietcong and the Gulf of Tonkin incident of 1964 (see page 70) confirmed the fears of many Americans about the domino theory of Communist expansion in South-East Asia. Should Vietnam fall it would be followed by countries such as Cambodia and Laos.

ACTIVITY ?

What can you learn from Source N about attitudes in the USA towards the war in Vietnam?

Source N A photograph published in a national newspaper in 1966. It shows President Johnson speaking to crowds in Indianapolis

The 'silent majority'

The 'silent majority' was a term first used in 1967 by George Meany, the leader of labor union federations in the United States. He was describing those members of unions, including himself, who supported the war as 'the vast, silent majority in the nation'. This was further publicised by Nixon in a speech he made in November 1969. By the 'silent majority' he was referring to the Americans who did not participate in the anti-war demonstrations. Nixon believed the opponents of the war dominated the media which gave little publicity to the many supporters of the war.

He was mainly referring to the middle aged and elderly all over America, more especially those who had served in the Second World War, as well as young people throughout the USA who eventually did service in Vietnam.

▲ **Source O** Cartoon published in an American newspaper in 1970, commenting on Nixon and the 'silent majority'

Source P An extract from Nixon's 'silent majority' speech of November 1969

So tonight, to you, the great silent majority of my fellow Americans, I ask for your support. I pledged in my campaign for the Presidency to end the war in a way that we could win the peace. I have initiated a plan of action which will enable me to keep that pledge. The more support I can have from the American people, the sooner that pledge can be redeemed. For the more divided we are at home, the less likely the enemy is to negotiate in Paris. Let us be united for peace. Let us also be united against defeat. Because let us understand: North Vietnam cannot defeat or humiliate the United States. Only Americans can do that.

ACTIVITIES ?

1 Study Source P. Why do you think Nixon gave this speech?

2 Working in pairs put together a reply to Nixon's speech (Source R) from those who opposed the war. This could be a speech or a newspaper article.

The 'hard hats'

Large numbers in the building and construction unions supported Nixon's Vietnam policy and were nicknamed the 'hard-hats'. Nixon claimed they were supporting 'freedom and patriotism'. One of the strongest supporters of the president's war policy was Peter J. Brennan. Brennan was president of the Building and Construction Trades Council of Greater New York, an alliance of building and construction unions in the New York City area.

Hard Hat riot, 8 May 1970

Shortly after the Kent State University shootings (see page 90), anti-war protesters announced they would hold a demonstration in order commemorate the four dead students. The hard hats retaliated by setting up their own rally of construction workers in order to demonstrate that they supported the policies of the Nixon administration. On the morning of 8 May, there was a protest by students in Manhattan, New York against the Kent State University shootings. However, about 200 construction workers attacked these students, beating up some of them with their hard hats. Witnesses suggested that the police did little or nothing to stop these attacks. More than 70 people were injured, including four policemen, but only six people were arrested.

> ### Practice question
>
> How useful are Sources P and Q for an enquiry into those who supported the war? Explain your answer, using Sources P and Q and your knowledge of the historical context. (*For guidance, see pages 71–73.*)

▼ **Source Q** The Hard Hat riots of 8 May 1970. The riots were widely publicised in the media

12.3 Causation question

This section provides guidance on how to answer the causation question.

Question 1

Explain why there was growing opposition to the US involvement in the war in Vietnam.

> You may use the following in your answer:
> - The media
> - US methods of warfare
>
> You **must** also use information of your own.

(12 marks)

How to answer

- Ensure you do not simply describe the two given points.
- Focus on the key words in the question, for example the theme of the question, which is causation, and any dates.
- Make use of at least the two given points and one of your own, or develop at least three points of your own.
- Write an introduction that identifies the key areas you are going to explain in your answer.

The diagram on page 95 shows the steps you should take to write a good answer to this question. Use the steps and examples to complete an answer to the question by writing paragraphs on each point (your own and those given) and linking them where possible. Alternatively you could use the flowchart below to structure your answer to the question.

INTRODUCTION
- Explain the key theme of the question.
- Suggest the key areas you are going to cover in your answer.

FIRST PARAGRAPH – FIRST GIVEN REASON (OR REASON OF YOUR OWN)
- Introduce the first reason.
- Fully explain this reason.

SECOND PARAGRAPH – SECOND GIVEN REASON (OR REASON OF YOUR OWN)

THIRD PARAGRAPH – REASON OF YOUR OWN (OR GIVEN REASON IF NOT YET COVERED)

STEP 1
Write an introduction that identifies the key reasons you need to cover in your answer and your main argument.

Example
In the later 1960s there was growing opposition to US involvement in the war in Vietnam. This was due to number of reasons including the influence of the media, US methods of warfare and the draft system.

STEP 2
Write at least one good length paragraph for at least three reasons.
For each paragraph:
• Introduce the reason (green in the example).
• Fully explain it (blue in the example).

Example
The first reason for the growth of opposition to the war in Vietnam was the influence of the media and more especially television.
The war in Vietnam was the first to be televised in great detail. Moreover, in the mid and late 1960s, colour television became readily accessible, which worsened the bloody nature of what was shown. The conflict was in the living rooms of most US families. This, together with photographs, revealed the brutality of the conflict and showed the appalling injuries caused by the use of napalm on civilians, including children.
This was very important because the media and in particular television highlighted American casualties, the effects of chemical weapons used by the USA and seemed to show that the USA had little hope of winning the conflict.

STEP 3
Now do the same for the second reason.

Example
A further reason for the growth of opposition to US involvement in the war in Vietnam was the American methods of warfare.

STEP 4
Complete this paragraph and write one more paragraph on another reason.

Question 2

Explain why there was support for US involvement in the war in Vietnam.

You may use the following in your answer:
■ Fear of communism
■ Hard Hats
You **must** also use information of your own.

ACTIVITY

Now have a go answering Question 2 using the steps shown for Question 1.

13 The peace process and end of the war

The USA began peace negotiations with North Vietnam as early as 1968. Nixon began to withdraw troops in 1969 due to his policy of Vietnamisation (see page 80). However, the peace negotiations dragged on for several years because each side stuck to its position, with the North only agreeing to peace if both Vietnams were reunited, while the USA would only agree to a peace which kept South Vietnam as a separate country. The North also insisted that the communist National Liberation Army should form part of a new government in the South. Agreement on these differences was not made until 1973 when, in March, the last American troops left Vietnam. This left a weakened South Vietnam which was unable to prevent occupation from the North and led to the eventual reunification of Vietnam in 1975.

13.1 The peace process

The peace negotiations between the USA and North Vietnam dragged on for several years until the signing of the Paris Peace agreement in January 1973.

Peace negotiations, 1968–73

Following the Tet Offensive in 1968 (see page 78), President Johnson suggested peace negotiations should begin and, much to his surprise, the North Vietnamese accepted his offer. Talks began, Johnson halted the bombing of North Vietnam and was hopeful that a peace agreement could be negotiated in a reasonable amount of time.

For months there was absolutely no progress in the talks, as each side haggled over minor issues, such as the shape and size of the meeting table, where people would sit, who would be in meetings, whether or not they would have small flags on the table and other petty issues. One major issue confronting the negotiators was the inclusion of the South Vietnamese communists as a separate negotiating group. South Vietnamese President Thieu did not want them at any meetings because he knew this gave the Vietcong legal status. The Vietcong had no form of government, no recognised leader and had disrupted life in South Vietnam. Nonetheless, they were granted an official position at the table.

Neither side was prepared to move from their stance and no progress was made for several months. In July of 1969, in an effort to move the talks forward, President Nixon authorised Henry Kissinger, US National Security Adviser, to open secret negotiations with the North Vietnamese only. Nixon was hopeful that they could make advances without the other two parties' direct involvement. Still the talks went nowhere and each side continued military action to try to improve its negotiating position.

The demands of each side

The initial positions of each side are summarised in Table 13.1 on page 97.

Perhaps the biggest stumbling block to the peace talks for the Americans was, ironically enough, the peace movement in the USA. The North Vietnamese closely followed the protests and riots in the USA and would read US newspaper articles to the US diplomats whenever they met. Their message was consistent – the US public would force their own troops out of Vietnam and the North need only wait them out. University demonstrations and protests, together with a biased press, resulted in the USA's negotiating team becoming virtually powerless. For nearly four years, the peace talks stuttered and meandered with no major breakthroughs.

Breakthrough in negotiations

The whole peace movement changed when Nixon visited China in February 1972. Both China and the Soviet Union, the two major communist countries at the time, were supporting North Vietnam, but neither country necessarily trusted the other. Nixon's trip helped to exploit the divisions between China and the Soviet Union, as well as the divisions between China and Vietnam. USA–Soviet Union relations had improved following the Moscow summit in May 1972 when Nixon became the first US president to visit the Soviet capital. The leader of the Soviet Union, Leonid Brezhnev, and his advisers acted as intermediary between Hanoi and Washington. This was a period in the Cold War known as *détente*, which saw an improvement in relations. Brezhnev used his role in Vietnam not only to further enhance *détente* and improve relations with America but also to show that the Soviet Union had a more influential position over Vietnam than China.

▼ **Table 13.1** Demands of the four sides in the peace negotiations

USA		North Vietnam	
Wanted the withdrawal of US and North Vietnamese forces from South Vietnam		Demanded the USA remove its forces immediately and unconditionally	
Hoped to allow the South Vietnamese people to work out their own political problems without influence or invasion from North Vietnam		Requested resignation of President Thieu	
Wanted all prisoners of war released			
South Vietnam		**South Vietnam communists (Vietcong)**	
Demanded the immediate and unconditional removal of North Vietnamese forces		Demanded the immediate removal of US forces	
Wanted South Vietnam to have one leader, not a coalition government		Vietcong forces must be allowed to stay in positons already under their control	
		Requested resignation of President Thieu	

The Paris Peace Agreement, 1973

An agreement was reached in October 1972 – Nixon was happy with the timing because it came just before the presidential elections. If the war ended, it would be a great achievement for Nixon.

In the terms of the October agreement:

- North Vietnam dropped its demand that President Thieu be replaced by a coalition.
- Nixon and Kissinger agreed to allow the North Vietnamese Army to remain in the areas they controlled.
- The Vietcong were to be allowed to participate in the final settlement.
- A ceasefire agreement was reached and the USA agreed to withdraw all remaining troops.
- All US prisoners of war would be repatriated.

President Thieu rejected the agreements because he knew that the USA was about to abandon him. Talks were halted in December, and some of Kissinger's staff even suggested having Thieu assassinated. Nixon was aware that **Congress** would not grant him funds for the war in 1973 and therefore the bombing campaign began on 18 December 1972 to force North Vietnam to finally agree to peace terms (see page 83).

On 23 January 1973, a ceasefire was signed in Paris that essentially mirrored the agreement of October 1972. This time President Thieu had no choice but to sign it. The USA was leaving Vietnam. This agreement was presented as the best solution available. President Nixon and Kissinger also assured Thieu that the USA would continue to aid the South Vietnamese and that, if the agreement was violated by North Vietnam, help would be forthcoming. Thieu's continued objection was that North Vietnamese troops were permitted to remain in areas they controlled in the South. Moreover, Thieu felt that the sudden withdrawal of US forces would cripple the South's military strength, leaving them vulnerable if the North decided to violate the ceasefire. Nevertheless, on 27 January 1973 a formal agreement was signed and the war was over.

▲ **Source A** Le Duc Tho (right), leader of the North Vietnam delegation in Paris, and Henry Kissinger (left) at the Paris peace talks, November 1972

Peace terms

All parties pledged to 'respect the independence, sovereignty, unity, and territorial integrity of Vietnam as recognised by the 1954 Geneva Agreements on Vietnam' (see page 66). The USA agreed to continue its withdrawal of troops, which had started in 1969, leading to a complete withdrawal by 29 March 1973.

Significance of the Paris Peace Agreement

The Paris Peace Agreement was significant for several reasons. Kissinger and Le Duc Tho were awarded the 1973 Nobel Peace Prize. Kissinger accepted the prize, while Le Duc Tho declined it, saying his country was not yet completely at peace. Moreover the agreement officially ended American involvement in Vietnam.

However, the peace agreement did not end the war in Vietnam. Shortly after the USA left South Vietnam in March 1973, the ceasefire collapsed.

The ceasefire ends

Thieu was in an excellent position because of the armaments provided by the USA. However, despite losing land and equipment in 1973, the North Vietnamese launched a huge attack on the South in December 1974.

President Thieu asked US President Ford (who had succeeded Nixon) and the US Congress for $300 million and military equipment, and was infuriated when his request was denied. Thieu said that the North had received massive amounts of aid from China and the Soviet Union and he did not want to be left behind.

The North Vietnamese won a key victory on 11 March 1975 and dislodged South Vietnamese troops from provincial capital of Ban Me Thuot, the anchor of Saigon defences in the Central Highlands. As the communists drove towards Saigon virtually unopposed, Thieu pledged that his troops would defend it 'to the last bullet, the last grain of rice'. Surrender came a month later.

Vietnam re-united

When the end did come, Thieu's resignation was demanded by all sides, including his former allies in the USA, in order to make way for peace talks with the North Vietnamese. Thieu reluctantly stepped down on 21 April 1975 and left the country, but the talks never came. South Vietnam was overrun shortly after his departure and Saigon was captured by the North Vietnamese on 30 April 1975. The government of North Vietnam united both North and South Vietnam on 2 July 1976 to form the Socialist Republic of Vietnam.

ACTIVITIES

1 Working in pairs, look again at the demands of the four sides shown in Table 13.1 on page 97. Explain fully why each side made its own particular demands.

2 What is meant by the term 'biased press'?

3 What impact did anti-war demonstrations in the USA have on peace talks?

4 Look at the terms of the October agreement and Table 13.1 on page 97. Copy and complete the table below to show the successes and failures of each side in the negotiations.

USA		North Vietnam	
Successes	Failures	Successes	Failures

South Vietnam		South Vietnam communists (Vietcong)	
Successes	Failures	Successes	Failures

5 Use a flow chart to show the developments of in the war in Vietnam in the years 1968–75, including the peace negotiations, the peace agreement and the subsequent defeat of South Vietnam.

13.2 The economic and human costs of the war for the USA

The war had very significant economic and human costs for the USA.

Economic cost

US involvement in the war was very expensive. In 1964 the cost to the taxpayer was under half a billion dollars but, within four years, this had increased to $26.5 billion dollars. The war was the main contributor to the government's $26 billion deficit and to rising inflation in 1968. The US Treasury's warning that the war could not go on, together with taxpayer resentment, helped to convince Johnson that the escalation of the war must stop and Nixon that the war must end.

Human cost

There was also a terrible human cost for the USA with more than 50,000 American deaths in Vietnam and a further 300,000 wounded. In addition, many of the American troops became drug addicts. Hard drugs were available easily and cheaply in Vietnam from neighbouring Laos and Cambodia. Official army estimates put heroin use by American troops at 30 per cent.

More than three million men and women served in the Vietnam War and Table 13.2 shows the number killed and wounded. Not shown in the figures is the number of around 100,000 men who returned without one or more limbs. The war, therefore, touched many families in the USA. There was some bitterness about those people who avoided service, the 'draft dodgers', many of whom fled to Canada or Europe. It is worth noting that not one member of the US Congress lost a son in the war.

▼ Table 13.2 Casualties in the Vietnam War. These figures were compiled from official releases from each country. The Vietnam figures were released in 1995

Force	Killed in action	Wounded in action	Missing in action	Captured in action
US Forces	47,378 [1]	304,704 [2]	2,338 [3]	766 [4]
MRVN	223,748	1,169,763	NA	NA
South Korea	4,407	17,060	NA	NA
Australia	469	2,940	6	NA
Thailand	351	1,358	NA	NA
New Zealand	55	212	NA	NA

[1] There were an additional 10,824 non-hostile deaths from a total of 58,202

[2] Of the 304,704 wounded in action, 153,329 required hospitalisation

[3] This number decreases as remains are recovered and identified

[4] 114 died in captivity

ACTIVITY

?

Work in pairs and make a list of what you can learn about the Vietnam War from Table 13.2.

Relatives of soldiers

As is usual in war, the relatives of the soldiers were greatly affected by their participation. The armed forces had their own organisations that looked after wives and relatives of service personnel but some independent support groups were formed, such as The League of American Vietnam Prisoners and the National League of Families of American Prisoners Missing in South-East Asia. The groups tried to put pressure on the US government to be more pro-active in the search for those taken prisoner or missing in action.

Treatment of veterans

American soldiers returning to America may not have expected to be treated as heroes. However, they certainly did not expect to be treated as criminals or child murderers, as they sometimes were. Medical treatment for wounded or disabled veterans in the USA was poor. Many found it difficult to find jobs or to get their old jobs back – even though a government law made employers keep their jobs open for them. Source B shows a memorial sculpture to those who fought in the Vietnam War.

More American veterans have committed suicide since the war than were killed in the war itself. For them, the process of adjusting to peace-time was too difficult. They felt betrayed by a country which was embarrassed by them.

▲ **Source B** Bronze sculpture erected in Washington, DC, in honour of those who fought in the Vietnam War

---

Source C A description of the effects of Vietnam on war veterans

Some 700,000 veterans, women as well as men, have suffered psychological effects. It has been shown that they are far more likely than the rest of the population to suffer panic attacks, depression, drug addiction and to be divorced or unemployed. More US veterans have committed suicide since the end of the war than were actually killed in it.

Source D From an interview with a soldier who served in Vietnam. He remembers how, when he landed in the USA, he went for a drink in the airport bar. There some young people of his age – 18 or 19 years old – spoke to him

'You just got back from where?' one of the kids says.

'Vietnam.'

'How do you feel about killing all of those innocent people?' the woman asks me out of nowhere.

I didn't know what to say. The bartender got a little uptight. But, I didn't say anything. They told me when I got discharged from the army that I was going to get hassle. But, I didn't believe them.

'Excuse me,' I called the bartender over. 'Could I buy them all a drink?' I felt guilty. I did kill. I tried to make up for it somehow.

'We don't accept drinks from killers', the girl says to me.

Practice questions

1   What can you infer from Source B about attitudes to the war? (*For guidance, see page 79.*)

2   Give two things you can infer from Source C about the effects of the Vietnam War on those who were involved in it. (*For guidance, see page 79.*)

3   How useful are Sources C and D for an enquiry into the treatment of American soldiers when they returned to the USA? Explain your answer, using Sources C and D and your knowledge of the historical context. (*For guidance, see pages 71–73.*)

14 Reasons for the failure of the USA in Vietnam

Ultimately US involvement in the conflict in Vietnam failed. This was due partly to the strengths of the enemy – North Vietnam and the Vietcong – and their effective use of guerrilla tactics. However, it was also as a result of the weaknesses of the USA and the South Vietnamese. More especially, the failure of America to develop tactics which could effectively counter guerrilla warfare led to their failure in the conflict.

14.1 Strengths and weaknesses of the North Vietnamese/Vietcong

North Vietnam did have certain weaknesses, but their strengths brought eventual success against the South and the US.

Weaknesses

The North's weaknesses included the fact that not everyone in North Vietnam was enthusiastic about the war (see Sources A, B and C). There was a traditional hostility between the North and the South. They also lacked the air power and military resources of the USA.

> **Source A** From a quote by Trinh Duc, a communist who served in the Vietcong
>
> There was no way we could stand up to the Americans. Every time they came in force we ran from them. Then when they turned their back, we'd follow them. We practically lived on top of them, so they couldn't hit us with artillery and air strikes.

> **Source B** From an interview with Le Thanh, a communist who lived in North Vietnam during the war
>
> I also asked questions about why nobody was coming back from the South. It began to seem like an oven pit. The more young people who were lost there, the more they sent. There was even a kind of motto that the whole generation of army-age North Vietnamese adopted. They tattooed it on themselves and they sang songs about it – 'Born in the North to die in the South'.

> **Source C** From a letter sent by a soldier in the NVA to his girlfriend in South Vietnam, July 1971
>
> This terrible war makes so many strange thoughts race through my head. I would like to jump up thousands of miles to get away from here, from killing. Before, I did not even know what it was like to kill a man. Now that I have seen it, I don't want to do it anymore. But it is the duty of a soldier to die for his country, me for our fatherland, the enemy for his. There is no choice.

ACTIVITY

What can you learn from Sources A, B and C about the strengths and weaknesses of North Vietnam and the Vietcong?

Practice questions

Give two things you can infer from Source A about guerrilla warfare. (*For guidance, see page 79.*)

Strengths

The Vietcong/North Vietnam had several strengths:

- In early 1965 the **Vietcong** had about 170,000 soldiers. The government of North Vietnam used **conscription** to maintain the size of its army. Every year, Hanoi sent 100,000 troops to the South. Women played an important role in the conflict, as shown by the female Vietcong patrol in Source D.
- They were fighting for two causes – communism and the reunification of Vietnam. Many in North Vietnam welcomed the chance to fight for the liberation of South Vietnam, as shown by Source E.
- They were prepared to accept a heavy body count. Between 500,000 and 900,000 died during the war.
- They knew the terrain and were skilled in guerrilla and jungle warfare.
- They won the support of the peasants of South Vietnam alienated by Diem's government and the USA's 'Search and Destroy' tactics.
- They were supplied by the Soviet Union and China with the necessary resources to fight the war. The Soviet Union provided 8,000 anti-aircraft guns and 200 anti-aircraft missile sites. Total assistance from the two countries has been estimated at over $2 billion between 1965 and 1968.
- Vietcong bases were well hidden and carefully booby-trapped to kill or wound US soldiers.
- They received support from the Soviet Union and China. Both countries supported the reunification of Vietnam under the communist North and supplied the North and Vietcong with rockets, tanks and fighter planes.
- The Ho Chi Minh trail provided vital supplies from the North of Vietnam to the Vietcong in the South (see page 69).

▲ **Source D** A female Vietcong patrol

Source E A North Vietnamese General speaking in 1967

In sending US troops to South Vietnam, the US imperialists have met a people's war. The people's war has succeeded in gathering all the people to fight their attackers in all ways and with all kinds of weapons.

ACTIVITY

Working in pairs, draw a set of scales with 'weaknesses of North Vietnamese/Vietcong' on one side and 'strengths of North Vietnamese/Vietcong' on the other.

a) One of you should summarise the North Vietnamese weaknesses, using page 101.

b) The other should summarise the North Vietnamese strengths, as described above.

c) Which way will the scale go? Why?

Practice questions

How useful are Sources D and E for an enquiry into the strengths of the North Vietnamese/Vietcong. Explain your answer, using Sources D and E and your knowledge of the historical context. (*For guidance, see pages 71–73.*)

14.2 Strengths and weaknesses of the US armed forces

Strengths

The USA had many strengths:

- Almost unlimited economic resources. The USA could access the most advanced technology as well as using the South Vietnamese forces.
- The USA had control of the air and could deploy this in a variety of ways including troop support, bombing and raids.
- Theoretically the USA had an almost unlimited numbers of troops. Around 2.8 million Americans served in Vietnam during the war. Two million of them were recruited by conscription or through the draft system.

Weaknesses

However, the USA also had many weaknesses:

- It had no experience or knowledge of guerrilla/jungle warfare carried out by the Vietcong.
- This inexperience was worsened by the fact that most of the US troops, especially after 1967, were not full combat troops but men (19 was the average age) who were drafted into the armed forces and generally served only one year in Vietnam. Of those killed in combat, 43 per cent died in the first three months of their tour of duty. Men found it difficult to get to know each other and work as a unit. No sooner had they learned the skills of survival and combat than their tour of duty ended.
- There was great hostility between officers and men. The officers were often professional soldiers who wanted a successful combat record to earn promotion. They had little empathy with young soldiers who simply wanted to survive their one-year tour of duty. This often led to 'fragging' or the killing of officers by the troops. During 1970–71, there were over 700 cases of 'fragging'.
- Some troops started using 'recreational drugs', such as marijuana, to see out their tour of duty. In 1971, 5,000 men were treated in hospital for combat wounds and 20,000 for drug abuse. Between 1966 and 1973 there were 503,000 cases of desertion in the US army in Vietnam.
- The public were not prepared to accept a heavy body count in Vietnam. In other words, the USA could not sustain the casualty rate of the Vietcong due to public opinion.
- Few of the troops believed they were defending democracy or even cared. Their main aim was reaching DEROS (Date Eligible for Return Overseas).
- There was growing opposition to the war in the USA (see pages 85–90) and this did little to raise the morale of the troops.

- The USA failed to win over the peasants of South Vietnam, who generally viewed the Americans as invaders and chose to support the Vietcong.
- US tactics such 'Search and Destroy' and chemical warfare failed to destroy the morale of the people of North Vietnam. If anything, it increased their determination to carry on the war.
- The morale of the US troops was badly affected by the deaths and injuries caused by enemy booby traps (see pages 74) and mine traps.

> **Source F** From an article in a British newspaper in January 1973
>
> By 1968, the USA had an army of over half a million men in South Vietnam. Over 36,000 had been killed there. American people were convinced that victory in Vietnam was not worth 300 American dead a week and $30,000 million a year. Television images showing the coffins of dead American soldiers encouraged even greater opposition to the war. More and more US citizens were convinced that this was a conflict they could not win.

> **Source G** From M. Bilton, *Four Hours in My Lai*, published in 1992. The author describes some of the US recruits
>
> An increasing number of recruits scored so low on the standard intelligence tests that they would have been excluded from the normal peacetime army. A rookie army which constantly rotated its inexperienced men was pitted against experienced guerrillas on their home ground.

ACTIVITIES

1 What can you learn from Source F about the reasons for the growth of opposition to US involvement in the war in Vietnam in the years after 1968?

2 Once again working in pairs, draw a set of scales with 'Weaknesses of US armed forces' on one side and 'Strengths of US armed forces' on the other.
   a) One of you should summarise the US weaknesses.
   b) The other should summarise the US strengths.
   c) Which way will the scale go? Why?

Practice question

Give two things you can infer from Source G about the US army in Vietnam. (*For guidance, see page 79.*)

14.3 The impact of opposition to the war in the USA

There is much debate whether US opposition to the war was the main reason for its defeat.

A great impact?

Some argue that opposition played an important role in weakening the US war effort and in bringing an end to US involvement. Due to the unpopularity of the war Johnson decided in 1968 that he would not seek re-election as president. His successor, Richard Nixon, won the presidential election mainly because he promised to 'end the war and win the peace'. In 1969, in order to reduce opposition, he introduced a policy of **Vietnamisation** (see page 80) that included the gradual withdrawal of US troops from the conflict.

A limited impact?

Others argue that the impact of opposition to the war may not have been as great as has been claimed, for several reasons:

- Protesters were easy to label as communists. To the majority of Americans they were traitors and cowards. Some historians even claim that the students simply alienated many Americans.
- The level of opposition to the war was not as great as claimed. In 1964, 85 per cent of Americans supported the government policy in the war. Even as late as 1970, after the invasion of Cambodia, a Gallup opinion poll showed 50 per cent approved of the invasion and only 35 per cent opposed it.
- Not all students protested against the war. Only 10 per cent of higher education institutions had serious anti-war disturbances and, within those 10 per cent, fewer than 10 per cent of students took part.
- Some even claim that television increased support for the war.

Overall the impact of the anti-war movement may have been exaggerated. Nevertheless, it certainly divided US public opinion and contributed to the eventual failure of US policy in Vietnam.

▲ **Source H** Protestors marching against the Vietnam War

ACTIVITIES

Which view do you agree with about the impact of opposition to the war – great or limited?

Practice questions

1   Give two things you can infer from Source H about opposition to the war in Vietnam. (*For guidance, see page 79.*)
2   Explain why the US lost the war in Vietnam.

You may use the following in your answer:
- The guerrilla tactics
- The US troops

You **must** also use information of your own.

(*For guidance, see pages 94–95.*)

14.4 Further examination practice on interpretations

Here is an opportunity to practise answering some more interpretation questions.

Source A General Westmoreland, who commanded the US forces in Vietnam until 1968, gave his views on the US media in 1979

Actions by opponents of the war in the United States were supported by the news media. The media, no doubt, helped to back up the message that the war was 'illegal' and 'immoral'. Then came the enemy's Tet Offensive of early 1968. The North Vietnamese and Vietcong suffered a military defeat. Despite this, reporting of the offensive by the press and television in the USA gave the impression of an endless war that could never be won.

Source B From *Selected Writings*, Ho Chi Minh, published in 1977. He explains the use of guerrilla tactics

When fighting in an enemy-occupied area, we must use guerrilla tactics. We must absolutely not go in for large-scale battles and big victories unless we are certain of success. The aim of guerrilla warfare is to nibble at the enemy, harass him in such a way that he can neither eat nor sleep in peace, to allow him no rest, to wear him out physically and mentally, and finally to annihilate him. Wherever he goes, he should be attacked by our guerrillas, stumble on land mines or be greeted by sniper fire.

Interpretation 1 From *Rise and Fall of the Great Powers*, P. Kennedy, published in 1988

Economically, the USA was 50 to 100 times more productive than North Vietnam. Militarily, it had the firepower to bomb the enemy back into the Stone Age. But this was not a war in which that superiority could be made effective. Fighting was reduced to a series of small-scale encounters in jungles and paddy fields. Moreover, the North Vietnamese and Vietcong were fighting for what they believed very strongly. The South Vietnamese government, by contrast, appeared corrupt and unpopular.

Interpretation 2 From *Access to History Context: An Introduction to American History, 1860–1990*, A. Farmer and V. Sanders, published in 2002

Some Americans, especially Vietnam War veterans, blame unsympathetic media coverage for the United States' failure to win in Vietnam. Initially the media were pro-war. However, as the lack of progress became evident to reporters in Vietnam, the media began to turn against the war. Tet accelerated that process. While the media did not cover Communist atrocities, reporters saw enough of South Vietnam to know there was something wrong with the Saigon regime and that American policy in supporting it was not always admirable.

Question 1

Study Interpretations 1 and 2. They give two views about the reasons for the failure of the USA to win in Vietnam. What is the main difference between the views? Explain your answer, using details from both interpretations.

- You need to give the views of each interpretation and back these up with evidence from each one.

Question 2

Suggest **one** reason why Interpretations 1 and 2 give different views about the reasons for the failure of the USA to win in Vietnam. You may use the sources to help explain your answer.

The interpretations may differ because:
- they have given weight to two different sources. You can use evidence from Sources A and B for this answer. Match the sources to the interpretations
- they are partial extracts and in this case they do not actually contradict one another
- the authors have a different emphasis.

Question 3

How far do you agree with Interpretation 2 about the reasons for the failure of the USA to win in Vietnam? Explain your answer, using both interpretations and your knowledge of the historical context.

You need to give a balanced answer which agrees and disagrees with the interpretation using evidence from the two interpretations as well as your own knowledge.
- Agree with the view with evidence from Interpretation 2.
- Agree with the view with evidence from your own knowledge.
- Disagree with the view with evidence from Interpretation 1.
- Disagree with the view with evidence from your own knowledge.
- Make a final judgement on the view.

Revise and practise

1 The position of black Americans in the early 1950s

Explain in no more than two sentences what you know about the following:

- segregation
- discrimination
- CORE
- NAACP

2 Progress in education

1 Decide whether the following statements are causes or effects of *Brown v Topeka* and Little Rock High School.

Statement	Cause	Effect
Linda Brown's parents wanted her to attend a neighbourhood school.		
Some areas began to desegregate by 1957.		
Lawyers from the NAACP led by Thurgood Marshall presented evidence to the Supreme Court.		
Many US citizens saw for the first time, at Little Rock, the racial hatred that existed in the Southern states.		
Nine black students tried to enroll at Little Rock High School but were prevented by the governor.		
Little Rock involved the president, demonstrating that civil rights was an issue that could no longer be ignored.		

2 Choose one of the following interpretations about the US education system in the 1950s and write a paragraph justifying the statement.
- There was considerable change in the US education system in the 1950s.
- There was some change in the US education system in the 1950s.
- There was little change in the US education system in the 1950s.

3 Which of the statements best sums up the success of the Montgomery Bus Boycott? Give reasons for your decision.
- It succeeded because of the car-pooling.
- It succeeded because of Martin Luther King.
- The Supreme Court intervened.

3 The Montgomery Bus Boycott and its impact

Make a copy of the table and decide the importance of each of the events in the Montgomery Bus Boycott. Explain your choice.

	Of little importance	Quite important	Important	Very important
Rosa Parks				
Jo Ann Robinson				
Montgomery Improvement Association (MIA)				

4 Opposition to the civil rights movement

Explain, in no more than two sentences, the importance of the following in the civil rights movement of the 1950s.

- The Ku Klux Klan
- The Dixiecrats
- The murder of Emmet Till

5 Progress, 1960–62

1 Summarise in no more than 20 words the importance of the following in the civil rights campaigns.
- Direct action
- Sit-in
- Freedom Riders
- James Meredith

2 'The Freedom Rides were a complete success.' Write two paragraphs disagreeing with this statement.

6 Peaceful protests and their impact, 1963–65

1 The following account about events in Birmingham is by a student who has not revised thoroughly. Rewrite the account, correcting any errors.

King decided to March to Birmingham in 1964 and in August the demonstrations began. King was arrested and he wrote his famous 'Article from Birmingham Prison'. On his release, President Kennedy sent troops and an agreement was reached to end segregation in Birmingham. At the end of the trouble Evers Medgar, a leader of CORE, was shot.

2 What explanation can you give for the following statements?
   - The march on Washington was a success.
   - Malcolm X was correct when he called the march the 'farce on Washington'.

3 Place the following events in chronological order:
   - Voting Rights Act
   - 'Freedom Summer'
   - Civil Rights Act
   - Assassination of President Kennedy
   - Assassination of Martin Luther King
   - Murder of civil rights activists Chaney, Goodman and Schwerner
   - Selma marches

7 Malcolm X and Black Power

Summarise in no more than 20 words the importance of each of the following in the civil rights movement in the 1960s.
- Malcolm X
- Black Power
- Black Panthers
- The death of Martin Luther King

8 The civil rights movement, 1965–75

1 Explain why each of the following was important in the civil rights movement.
   - The riots of 1965–67
   - The Kerner Report

2 'The civil rights campaigns had been a complete success by 1975.' Write **two** paragraphs disagreeing with this statement.

9 Reasons for US involvement in Vietnam, 1954–63

1 Summarise in no more than 20 words the importance of each of the following in increased US involvement in Vietnam.
   - Dien Bien Phu
   - The Geneva Agreement
   - Ngo Dinh Diem
   - Vietcong
   - Strategic Hamlets Policy
   - Domino Theory

2 The following account of the Gulf of Tonkin incident is by a student who has not revised thoroughly. Re-write the account, correcting any errors.

On 2 August 1966 the US aircraft carrier Maddox was fired at by South Vietnamese patrol boats in the Gulf of Tonkin. The Maddox was gathering intelligence information. Two months later there was a second alleged attack. Evidence later showed this did not happen. Johnson was not able to use these attacks to persuade Congress to support greater US involvement.

10 The nature of the conflict in Vietnam, 1964–68

1 Are the following statements about the Vietnam War true or false?

Statement	True	False
The Vietcong used Search and Destroy tactics		
The Vietcong used a system of tunnels		
The USA launched Operation Rolling Thunder in 1967		
The USA used chemical weapons such as napalm		
The Vietcong were supplied through the Ho Chi Minh Trail		

2 Choose one of the following interpretations of the tactics used in the Vietnam War and write a paragraph justifying the statement.
   - The USA used effective tactics against the Vietcong in Vietnam
   - The USA used ineffective tactics against the Vietcong in Vietnam
   - The USA were successful in dealing with guerrilla warfare in Vietnam

11 Changes under Nixon, 1969–73

1 Explain, in no more than a sentence, what you know about the following:

Vietnamisation   Bombing of North Vietnam   Invasion of Laos

The Nixon Doctrine   Bombing of Cambodia

2 Place the following in chronological order:
- The bombing of North Vietnam
- The invasion of Laos
- The introduction of Vietnamisation
- The bombing of Cambodia

12 Attitudes to the war in the USA

1 Correctly pair the sentences in the table.

The My Lai Massacre took place in March 1968.	The aim was to identify and arrest at least 3,000 Vietcong suspects each month.
The Kent State University shootings occurred in 1970.	The workers chose those with the longest hair and beat them with their hard hats.
In 1968 the US Central Intelligence Agency (CIA) set up 'Operation Phoenix'.	Four students were shot dead by National Guardsmen.
In May 1970 the Hard Hat Riot took place.	A platoon of American soldiers massacred a village in South Vietnam.

2 Draw a series of concentric circles. Categorise the importance of the following reasons for the growth of opposition to US involvement in the War in Vietnam and place the most important in the centre of your circle, working out to the least important on the outside.
- The media
- The draft system
- The Tet Offensive
- US methods of warfare

13 The peace process and end of the war

Summarise, in no more than 20 words, the part played by the following in the peace negotiations between the USA and North Vietnam.
- Henry Kissinger
- Nixon's visit to China in 1972
- President Thieu

14 Reasons for the failure of the USA in Vietnam

1 For the following two statements, write two or three sentences agreeing with the statement.

Opposition to the war in the USA had a significant impact on the American defeat

Opposition to the war in the USA had a limited impact on the American defeat

2 Was the defeat of the USA in Vietnam due to American weaknesses or the strengths of the Vietcong? Draw a Venn diagram, with 'American weaknesses' on the left circle, 'combination of the two', where the two circles intersect, and 'Vietcong strengths' on the right circle.

Glossary

armistice   When, during a war, a treaty is signed by the different sides to seal the end of combat

artillery   Large field guns, mortars or cannons

Attorney General   Chief legal officer of the US government

Black Panther Party   An extreme group of black nationalists who believed that black Americans should arm themselves and force the whites to give them equal rights

capitalism   A belief in private ownership of the means of creating wealth, such as industry and agriculture

Central Intelligence Agency (CIA)   The US office which coordinates and conducts espionage and intelligence activities

civil war   A war between two different groups in the same country

Cold War   The opposite of a hot or actual war. A propaganda war between the USA and the Soviet Union in the years after 1945 which increased tension between the Superpowers

colonial empires   Refers to parts of the world taken over by larger powers

Communism   A system which puts forward a classless society where private ownership has been abolished and the means of production and subsistence belong to the community

Congress   The US equivalent of parliament. Congress is split into two parts – the Senate and the House of Representatives

congressmen   Members of Congress

Congress of Racial Equality (CORE)   Established in 1942 by James Farmer. CORE was the first organisation in the USA to use the tactic of sit-ins

conscription   Where males of a certain age (usually 18–41) have to serve in the armed forces for a period of time. Containment Using US influence and military resources to prevent the expansion of communism into noncommunist countries

containment   Using US influence and military resources to prevent the expansion of communism into non-communist countries

conventional methods of warfare   Warfare conducted without nuclear weapons

coup d'état   An armed rebellion or revolt against the existing government

defoliants   Chemicals sprayed on plants to remove their leaves

democratic republic   A country ruled by a popularly elected president

desegregation   Removal of the policy of segregation

détente   A reduction in the tension between the USA and the Soviet Union during the Cold War

discrimination   Unfair treatment of individuals because of their gender, race or religious beliefs

Dixiecrats   Democrat Party senators from the southern states

draft   The US name for conscription. It was compulsory for men who reached the age of eighteen to serve in the armed forces

enfranchise   To give an individual the right to vote

Federal Government   The central government of the USA, based in Washington, DC

filibuster   Obstructing or delaying a piece of legislation by making long speeches or introducing irrelevant issues

Freedom Schools   Temporary, alternative free schools for African Americans, mostly in the South. They were part of a nationwide effort during the civil rights movement to organise African Americans to achieve social, political and economic equality

ghettoes   A densely populated area of a city inhabited by a socially and economically deprived minority

gooks   The US nickname for the people of Vietnam, especially the Vietcong

'Great Society'   A set of domestic programmes enacted in the USA on the initiative of President Johnson. A main focus was to end poverty and racial injustice

guerrilla   Someone who fights in a guerrilla war

guerrilla warfare   Fighting in small groups against conventional forces, using such methods as sabotage, sudden ambush, etc.

inauguration speech   The speech given by a president at his swearing-in ceremony (inauguration)

Ku Klux Klan   A secret society of white people in the American south who believed in white supremacy and resorted to violence against black people as well as Jews and other minority groups

lynching   When a mob kills someone for a cause they believe in, without the due process of law

mobile war   A war in which the armed forces are on the move usually in armoured vehicles, tanks, helicopters or aeroplanes

napalm   An inflammable sticky jelly used in bombs in order to set fire to people, trees and buildings

National Association for the Advancement of Colored People (NAACP)   A pressure group founded in 1909 that lobbies to eliminate racial hatred and racial discrimination

Nation of Islam   A group founded in 1931, which aimed to provide black Americans with an alternative to Christianity and to keep blacks and whites separate. It did not teach the orthodox Islamic faith

National Liberation Front (NLF)   A political organisation and army in South Vietnam and Cambodia that fought the US and South Vietnamese governments during the Vietnam War. Also known as the Vietcong

New Frontier   A slogan used by John F. Kennedy to describe his aims and policies. He maintained that, like the Americans of the frontier in the nineteenth century, Americans of the twentieth century had to rise to new challenges, such as achieving equality of opportunity for all

pitched battles   Battles fought in the open country between the armies of the two sides.

Red Scare   Term used in the USA after the communist revolution in Russia in 1917. It wa the fear that immigrants from Eastern Europe would bring to the USA ideas about a communist revolution

republic   A form of government in which the elected representatives, usually a president, have the power.

Republican   A supporter of the Republican Party, whose main ideas were to keep taxes low, limit the powers of the federal government, follow policies that favoured business and encourage self-sufficiency

Republican Party   One of the two main political parties in the USA. More conservative than their rival, the Democratic Party.

segregation   Separating groups due to their race or religion. This could include separate housing, education, health treatment, access to public building

segregationist   Those who believed in the policy of separation of races

Senate   The Upper House of the US Congress (parliament).

Senator   Member of the Senate. There are two senators per state

separatism   Keeping races apart

silent majority   A phrase used to describe the moderate people in society who are too passive to make their views known.

sit-in   A form of civil disobedience in which demonstrators occupy a public place and, as a protest, refuse to move.

Southern Christian Leadership Conference (SCLC)   African American civil rights group founded in 1957, whose first president was Martin Luther King

Southern Manifesto   A document written in the US Congress in 1956, opposing racial integration in education

Student Non-violent Co-ordinating Committee (SNCC)   A committee set up by black and white students in the USA to campaign for civil rights.

Superpowers   The name given to the USA and Soviet Union in the years after 1945, as they were clearly more economically and militarily powerful then the rest of the world.

Truman Doctrine   US President Truman's idea that it was the USA's duty to prevent the spread of communism to eastern Europe and the rest of the world. To do this, he was also prepared to engage the USA in military enterprises all over the world.

Vietcong   The communist-led guerrilla army and political movement whose aim was to topple the South Vietnamese government.

Vietminh   The League for the Independence of Vietnam, a nationalist, communist-dominated movement originally formed in 1941 to fight for Vietnamese independence from French rule.

Vietnamisation   The policy used by President Nixon to enable the USA to withdraw troops from Vietnam by getting the South Vietnamese to take on more responsibility for the war

White Citizens' Councils   Groups of white people who worked to maintain segregation

White supremacists   People who believed that white people were superior to black people

Index

Acknowledgements

The Publishers would like to thank the following for permission to reproduce copyright material:

Photo credits

p.6, **p.12** *t*, **p.40**, **p.102** Corbis; **p.7** © AS400 DB/Corbis; **p.9**, **p.15**, **p.32** © The Granger Collection / TopFoto; **p.11** *l* © Topeka State Journal, *r* © AP / Press Association Images; **p.12** *b* © Library of Congress (LC-U9- 2908-15); **p.16** *t, b*, **p.17** *l*, **p.19** © Don Cravens / The LIFE Images Collection / Getty Images; **p.17** *r* , **p.25**, **p.26**, **p.30** *l, r*, **p.33** *b*, **p.39** *r*, **p.47**, **p.51**, **p.54** *l*, **p.57**, **p.58**, **p.60**, **p.64**, **p.69**, **p.70** *l, r*, **p.76**, **p.84**, **p.86**, **p.97** © Bettmann / Corbis; **p.21** © Topham / AP / TopFoto; **p.23**, **p.67** © Everett Collection Historical / Alamy Stock Photo; **p.24** © Mary Evans / Everett Collection; **p.27** © AP / TopFoto; **p.29** *t* Jack Moebes / Corbis; **p.29** *b*, **p.56** © David J. Frent / David J. & Janice L. Frent Collection / Corbis; **p.33** *t* © Donald Uhrbrock / The LIFE Images Collection / Getty Images; **p.34** © Bill Mauldin, Library of Congress; **p.35** © Library of Congress, Yanker Poster Collection; **p.39** *l* © AP / TopFoto; **p.41** © Hulton-Deutsch Collection / Corbis; **p.42** © AP Photo / BH, File; **p.43** © MPI / Getty Images; **p.45**, **p.53** © Flip Schulke / Corbis; **p. 46**, **p.91** White House Photo / Alamy Stock Photo; **p. 54** *r* © Topham Pictures via TopFoto; **p.55** © Ted Streshinsky / Corbis; **p.63**, **p.77** © Larry Burrows / The LIFE Picture Collection / Getty Images; **p.65** © Sipa / Rex Features; **p.66**, **p.92** © Les Gibbard / University of Kent Cartoon Library; **p.68** © Pictorial Press Ltd / Alamy Stock Photo; **p.73** © Gib Crockett, Washington Star; **p.75** © Topham / Picturepoint; **p.81** © Oliphant / Universal Press Syndicate. Reprinted with permission. All rights reserved; **p.83** © Sovfoto / UIG via Getty Images; **p.85** © Philip Jones Griffiths / Magnum Photos; **p.87** © MPI / Getty Images; **p.88** © David Burnett / The LIFE Images Collection / Getty Images; **p.89** © World History Archive / Alamy Stock Photo; **p.90** © John Frost / Mirror; **p.93** © Leo Vals / Frederic Lewis / Archive Photos / Getty Images; **p.100** © Lee Snider / Photo Images / Corbis; **p.104** © J.P. Laffont / Sygma / Corbis.

Acknowledgements

p.10 R. Field, *Civil Rights in America 1865–190* (Cambridge University Press, 2002); **p.13** *l*, From C.N. Trueman, '1964 Civil Rights Act' www.historylearningsite.co.uk; *tr*, From www.humanrights.com/voices-for-human-rights/martin-luther-king-jr.html; *br* J. Martell, *The Twentieth Century World* (Nelson, 1985); **p.15** J.A. Gibson Robinson, *Montgomery Bus Boycott and the Women Who Started It: The Memoir of Jo Ann Gibson Robinson* (University of Tennessee Press, 1987); **p.17** M.L. King, *Stride Toward Freedom* (Harper & Brothers, 1958); **p.18**, **p.20** C. Carson (ed.), *The Papers of Martin Luther King Jr: Birth of a New Age* (University of California Press, 1955); **p.19**, **p.50** F. Powledge, *Free At Last? The Civil Rights Movement and the People Who Made It* (Harper Perennial, 1992); **p.22**, **p.36**, **p.49** M. Scott-Baumann and D. Platt, *Our Changing World: Modern World History from 1919* (Hodder Arnold, 1989); **p.22**, **p.36**, **p.49** P. Sauvain, *The Modern World 1914–80* (Stanley Thornes, 1989); **p.24** From an editorial in *The Chicago Defender* (national edn.) (1921–1967) Chicago, Ill. October 1, 1955, 'What Can You Do About the Disgrace in Sumner'; **p.25** *t* S.D. Cook, 'Political Movements and Organisations' (*Journal of Politics*, 1964); **p.30** *r* From a BBC/WGBH Boston broadcast 'Skin Deep Racial Oppression is Challenged in the United States and South Africa', original broadcast: Thursday, June 17, 1999; **p.31** V. Harding, *The Other American Revolution* (University of California Center for African Studies, 1980); **p.32** Bob Dylan 'Oxford Town' © 1963 by Warner Bros. Inc, permission granted by Special Rider Music – SESAC; **p.36** From http://spartacus-educational.com/USApantherB.htm; **p.36** From 'What We Want', article in *New York Review of Books* by Stokely Carmichael, September 22, 1966: www.nybooks.com/articles/1966/09/22/what-we-want/; **p.39** From www.pbs.org/wgbh/americanexperience/features/primary-resources/jfk-civilrights/; **p.40** From http://voicesofdemocracy.umd.edu/lewis-speech-at-the-march-on-washington-speech-text/; **p.44** From www.pbs.org/wgbh/americanexperience/features/primary-resources/jfk-civilrights/; **p.50** R. Green, L. Becker and R. Covello, *The American Tradition, A History of the United States* (Charles E Merrill, 1984); H. Ward, *World Powers in the Twentieth Century* (Heinemann, 1985); **p.52** *tl* A. Haley, *The Autobiography of Malcolm X* (Ballantine Books, NY, 1964); *bl* From www.malcolm-x.org/quotes.htm; *tr* From www.blackpast.org/1964-malcolm-x-s-speech-founding-rally-organization-afro-american-unity; *br* From www.malcolm-x.org/docs/abt_eulo.htm; **p.53** From http://spartacus-educational.com/USAcarmichael.htm; **p.54** *t* From http://spartacus-educational.com/CRsmithT.htm#source; **p.55** *t* From http://spartacus-educational.com/USApantherB.htm; *b* H. Newton, *Revolutionary Suicide* (Random House, 1973); **p.56** Quoted in R. Major, *A Panther is a Black Cat: An Account of the Early Years of the Black Panther Party – Its Origins, Its Goals, and Its Struggle for Survival* (Black Class Press, 2007); **p.57** From www.historycentral.com/documents/LBJwatts.html; **p.58** *l* From the Kerner Report, 1968; **p.59** *l*, **p.105** *b* A. Farmer and V. Sanders, *American History 1860–1990* (Hodder, 2011); *r* C. Carson, D.J. Garrow, G. Gill, V. Harding and D. Clark Hine (eds.) *The Eyes on the Prize Civil Rights Reader: Documents, Speeches, and First Hand Accounts from the Black Freedom Struggle* (Penguin, 1991); **p.66** *t, b* B. Walsh, *Modern World History* (Hodder, 2001); **p.70**, **p.74**, **p.76**, **p.77**, **p.78**, **p.79** *lb*, **p.86** *t*, **p.87**, **p.89** *l, r*, **p.100** *r*, **p.101**, **p.105** *t* N. DeMarco, *Vietnam 1939–75* (Hodder, 1998); **p.72** From www.presidency.ucsb.edu/ws/?pid=74176; **p.73** From www.nationalarchives.gov.uk/education/coldwar/G6/cs1/s3_t.htm; **p.74** *t*, **p.79** *r*, **p.103** *t* S. Waugh, *Essential Modern World History* (Nelson-Thornes, 2002); **p.80** From www.pbs.org/wgbh/americanexperience/features/primary-resources/nixon-vietnam/; **p.81** H.R. Haldeman, *The Ends of Power* (Times Books, 1978); **p.82** *t* From www.pbs.org/wgbh/americanexperience/features/primary-resources/nixon-asia/?flavour=mobile; *m* From an article 'A Cut-Off Date for War Funds', editorial in *St. Louis Post-Dispatch*, May 3, 1970; *b* R. Burks Verrone and L.M. Calkins, *Voices From Vietnam, Eye-witness Accounts of the War* (David & Charles, 2005); **p.90** *t* From www.presidency.ucsb.edu/ws/?pid=2496; *b* www.pbs.org/program/day-60s-died/; **p.92** From www.pbs.org/wgbh/americanexperience/features/primary-resources/nixon-vietnam/; **p.100** *l* S. Judges, *Superpower Rivalry* (Longman, 1984); **p.102** C. Culpin, *Making History* (Collins, 1996); **p.103** *b* M. Bilton, *Four Hours in My Lai* (Penguin, 1992); **p.105** Ho Chi Minh, *Selected Writings* (Foreign Languages Publishing House, 1977); **p.105** *m* P. Kennedy, *Rise and Fall of the Great Powers* (Random House USA Inc., 1988).

Every effort has been made to trace all copyright holders, but if any have been inadvertently overlooked, the Publishers will be pleased to make the necessary arrangements at the first opportunity.